STRATEGIC MOVES

Mind-Building Chess Exercises for Kids

CAROL ANN CARONIA

INTRODUCTION BY BRUCE PANDOLFINI

A POST HILL PRESS BOOK
ISBN: 979-8-88845-314-8
ISBN (eBook): 979-8-88845-315-5

Strategic Moves:
Mind-Building Chess Exercises for Kids

Cover design by Jim Villaflores

Post Hill Press
New York • Nashville
posthillpress.com

Published in the United States of America
1 2 3 4 5 6 7 8 9 10

This book is dedicated to all of my students,
who have taught me so much and given much joy.

CONTENTS

Introduction by Bruce Pandolfini 7
Preface 10

PART ONE

New People/Old People
or Assessing Performance 23
How to Find Your Name
or Analyzation 101 31
The Chessboard Is Not a Tablecloth
or Pattern Recognition 39
Make Your Own Chessboard
or Putting the Lesson into Action 49
What Is a Question?
or Developing Data 61
Mazes and Mistakes
or Analysis in Action 69
Partner vs. Opponent
or Competition 77
Never Believe Your Opponent
or Never Believe Your Opponent 85

Chess Values
or How to Decide What's Important 93

Chess Is a Big Numbers Game
or Game, Art, Science 101

How to Be a Good Winner
or Good Game. I had fun. 109

Touch Move
or Actions Have Consequences 115

PART TWO

Girls and Chess
or Stylistic Differences.................................. 125

Good Advice
or Learned from Experts 137

What Parents Should Not Do
or WARNING! WARNING!........................ 145

The Grand Finale 155

Acknowledgments.. 159

About the Author.. 160

INTRODUCTION

CHESS HAS A STORIED HISTORY and can be viewed in many ways. Some see it as a mental sport, others as a "tormental" game. All over the kaleidoscope of culture, from the thought experiments of Albert Einstein to the number-crunching calculus of Deep Blue, from the verbal truths of Shakespeare to the cinematic epiphanies of Ingmar Bergman, chess has left its indelible imprint on the intellectual landscape. Yet its abstruse reputation belies the truth. It's a game anyone can learn quickly and enjoy right away. Even so, it helps to get off to a soaring start, and that's where *Strategic Moves* by Carol Ann Caronia comes in.

For many years I've had the opportunity to work with this exceptional chess teacher. In various programs, teaching preschoolers to fifth graders, "Ms. Carol," as she is affectionately known, consistently shows how to galvanize young minds so they can achieve their full potential in chess—and in life. She's often the first to spot innate talent. It was Carol Ann who discovered and brought into the fold Fabiano Caruana, now the highest-ranked American chess player ever. I remember when she first pointed out Fabiano to me, when he was a mere five years old, and told me he was the real deal. She clearly knew what she was talking about.

But whether a student is gifted or not, I've always marveled at Carol Ann's genius for teaching and instruction. We often speak, and debate, about how to reach children, particularly in this current moment. Three years of COVID-19 have disrupted in-school learning, and test scores among younger students have dropped dramatically. So how do we inspire and encourage successful, long-term learning for children at home and at school? It is an art gifted to very few people, and as parents and teachers, we can spend our lives trying to figure it out. Carol Ann is an educator who possesses this rare quality. It's the reason she has become a long-standing figure, an institution at her places of teaching.

Carol Ann easily gets through to kids, regardless of who they are or where they came from. She has a real knack for motivating young girls to be assertive, while appreciating their own talents and strengths. It's astonishing how often a shy and withdrawn girl sheds protective skin to become proactive at the chessboard, and in practically everything else, under Ms. Carol's confidence-building tutelage. Long before the Netflix series *The Queen's Gambit*, Ms. Carol encouraged more than a few Beth Harmons to achieve their full potential.

I've always thought Ms. Carol's enlightened approach should be out there for everyone's edification, which brings us back to this one-of-a-kind book. In these chapters, she displays her virtuoso techniques, solving problem after problem, simultaneously imparting life lesson after life lesson. Sundry books show how to play chess, but rarely do we witness a veteran educator help students surmount stumbling blocks to learning in such smoothly concrete ways. Herein, Carol Ann Caronia distills a lifetime of on-the-job success into purified essence. Her personal enthusiasm and pragmatic toolbox almost always turn the conceptual into the tangible, and her cornucopia of didactic tricks seems inexhaustible.

Who can benefit from this remarkable book? Teachers, of course, and certainly parents, who are looking for ways to encourage successful, long-term learning in their children. But really, anyone wanting to sharpen problem-solving skills or to relearn the world's most universal game through new eyes, as well as the legion of binge-watchers stirred by the success of Netflix's *The Queen's Gambit* series. Almost everyone can derive rewards from this admirable offering. For one and all, *Strategic Moves* is simply a great read.

I've been teaching for many years, and though I've seen Carol Ann's methods put to effect in actual classrooms, reading through this book has given me greater awareness of how her sensitivity and inspired thinking enriches the lives of her students. Not only did I thoroughly enjoy perusing it, I plan to turn to it often as a reminder that, despite obstacles in the way of learning, there's always a path past them, especially when guided by the wisdom of a master teacher. My advice? Move ahead to the next page, discovering and digging into Carol Ann's strategic treasure trove of wisdom and insight.

Bruce Pandolfini
USCF National Master, Author, and Legendary Chess Teacher

PREFACE

I AM NOT A CHESS PLAYER. Let me be clear about that from the beginning. Not only am I not a grandmaster, I don't compete in tournaments and I never have. Despite all of that, I have had a long and successful career as an afterschool chess teacher. I've taught literally thousands of children in Brooklyn and Manhattan, most of them in Park Slope, where I have lived these many years. The vast majority of the students I've taught have been neighborhood kids. Many live across the street, or on my block, or around the corner. Through the years, I've watched the kids I once taught grow older, and eventually I'll see their younger brothers and sisters come to class after them. In one case, four children from one family attended my class over a span of ten years, the eldest leading the way. Chess, at least in my world, is a family affair, a neighborhood institution, and an international phenomenon, all wrapped into one.

Some of the kids I teach pass through my class for a semester and are gone. Some leave after one term and go to another class, then return again. Many kids stay with me or in the program I run with Bruce Pandolfini at The Berkeley Carroll School, all the way from pre-pre-K until fourth or fifth grade. A few kids return to help me teach the younger kids, or stay through high school as assistants. Ms. A—my former student, now colleague—has been with me from kindergarten through college and beyond. Like Ms. A, several others have become true friends. No matter which path they choose, I hope I've made a difference in each and every one of my students' lives for the better.

I am a teacher. It's not what I started out as, but as it turns out, teaching is what I am good at doing. It hasn't gotten me rich, or even made me a decent living, just an adequate one. There have never been sick days, or vacation days, or health insurance, or a pension plan. If I don't show up for work, I don't get paid, so I go to teach even if I feel crummy. "Afterschool," as you'll come to understand it, is market driven. If I don't do a good job, the kids don't choose my class. If the class isn't filled, the class isn't offered. I have to earn the trust and respect of each student, one satisfied parent, one more year of the class at a time. This is just one life lesson reflected in my teachings, and it's an important one.

Above and beyond that, however, my career as a chess teacher working with young children has been the most rewarding thing I have ever done, and had I the opportunity to do it over, I would choose the same path.

While I can't take full credit for the future success of my students, I like to think that I had a significant role in shaping their way of thinking, introducing them to a method of taking on real challenges to accept defeat, and how to be gracefully triumphant. At least three of my former students—Sean, Robert, and Fabiano—have done well in national and international chess competitions. All three began in my kindergarten class at Congregation Beth Elohim and attended my afterschool classes through grade school. Sean, a student of the PS 230 gifted program who attended my classes there, won the sixth grade national championship and is now a journalist. Robert, also a student at PS 230 who attended my classes there as well, won the sixth grade national team championship and is now a doctor. He actually returned to PS 230 while he was in high school to assist me in teaching my classes there. (Fun fact about Robert: when he was pre-med at Boston College, he delighted in popping over to Harvard and destroying their chess team. *Go Robert!*)

Fabiano, on the other hand, has been competing on the international stage since he and his family relocated to Italy after fifth grade. In 2018, Fabiano challenged World Chess Champion Magnus Carlsen for the world title. He's the only person in history to hold the sitting world champ to a hard-fought, all-draw match. He then went on to become the 2020/2023 US Chess Champion. In the chess world, Fabiano is famous.

I also have past students who have earned PhDs, MDs, MBAs. I still remain in touch with many of them to this day and follow their successes as if these kids were my own, not an uncommon practice when you've been a teacher as long as I have. One memorable former student, Adam, earned his doctorate in physics at the world-famous CERN—the European Laboratory for Particle Physics. Another particular standout, Julian, is now an international financier.

These are great accomplishments. For me, though, what's important is giving structure to my students' minds, teaching them logic, critical thinking, problem-solving. Those skills facilitate success, academic and otherwise.

Strategic Moves does not teach chess. There is nearly an uncountable number of books doing that. Instead, this book brings techniques to parents and others for instructing children to think in a structured, problem-solving manner, using chess as a model. For this reason, however, you, the reader, should be thoroughly versed in all chess rules and moves. If you need a refresher, look to the internet or to any of the various instructional books on chess. One of the great beauties of chess is that the rules never change. What does change is the way we think about chess itself.

In my chess classes, of course, I do teach the moves and the rules. I also teach students the proper way to win, and to lose. (I am of the firm opinion that good winners make for good losers, but more on that later.) what I am most earnest about though, is thinking, and *Strategic Moves* demonstrates how to educate students to gather information, assess that data, and come to good conclusions. These are skills all students must have to succeed not only in school, but in life. I want children to learn how to compete without bad feelings, and how to channel the aggressive urges of competition (about 95 percent of my students are aggressive little boys) into compassion for their opponents without losing a competitive edge. With my methods in place, you will be able to teach children how to compete hard without fear of offending a friendly opponent.

♟

Strategic Moves is being released at a critical time. In the past few years, the opportunities for non-traditional education and instruction have opened up and expanded like never before. If you are a parent, you are probably more involved in educating your children than you imagined was possible, with in-class teaching having been limited for more than a year, and homeschooling, micro schools, online teaching, and myriad combinations of these becoming more prominent.

Additionally, as we move away from standardized testing, there is a clearer emphasis on *how* we teach children, and how they can be successful. This emphasis is not going away any time soon. For generations, parents have accepted the set curricula of their children's schools without giving much input. But as test scores fall, educators and experts are encouraging parents and teachers to to be more involved in their kids' education. They should learn together, and focus on providing high-quality support so that their children gain the skills they need for a bright future. Afterschool and enrichment classes are one way to develop these essential skills. Books like *Strategic Moves* are another.

I intend to take you through processes, one by one—from the simplest lessons of how to measure a child's performance, to more advanced ones, such as how to teach them cause and effect (as presented in the chapter subtitled "Actions Have Consequences")—all through the wonderful, challenging, fascinating lens of chess. Once students have these invaluable skills, they will be able to master any subject, empowered with the proper tools to make good decisions and to understand how information from one lesson can be applied in other areas.

You probably remember the old saying: "As the twig is bent, so the tree will grow." Through years of teaching, I have found this to be true. Drawing on my experiences, I hope I can provide insights to teachers and mentors of all stripes, helping them empower children to think for themselves, to apply logic, to make good decisions, and—above all—*to learn how to learn.*

Despite my years of success as an afterschool teacher, it might surprise you to learn that just as I am not a chess player, I am also not a certified teacher. I have no degree in education; in fact, I took not one education course in college. I attended St. John's University, with a major in English—the course of choice for those who have no clear idea what they are going to do upon graduation.

I invented my method of study in high school, and I made it more intense in college: ask questions, then understand and digest what the instructor was trying to convey. I asked so many questions the professor's irritation was sometimes palpable. Needless to say, when it came to my years in school, I had great fun.

One of the most memorable courses at St. John's was Logic. I remember it vividly because the professor was a terrible teacher. I can still see him, young and scraggly, standing at the blackboard (yes, this was before the age of Chromebooks, projectors, and even whiteboards), talking in circles and writing incomprehensibly and barely looking at the students in the class. Just about everybody in the class did miserably. Asking him questions was an exercise in frustration, as it was never clear if he had, indeed, answered.

I managed to pull off a B or B+ (probably marked on a curve), just because I was much more determined than most of my other classmates to learn what the heck he was trying to convey. The main lesson I took away was this syllogism:

> **If all As are Bs, and all Bs are Cs, then all As are Cs.**

There was also one which stated that all As, some As, and no As are—or are not, or may possibly be—Bs and/or Cs (that is, *some* As are Bs, which implies that *some* As are *not* Bs). It was perhaps far more complicated than what I have presented here, but I digress. What I do know is that even this half-remembered construct has helped me think more clearly than I might have, had I not taken the course—terrible professor be damned.

Chess, of course, is logic, in its purest, most practical form. Chess-playing computers demonstrate this as they run through impossibly high numbers of possibilities at warp speed: if this, then that. To play chess well, to win more than you lose, you must be able to assess potential moves and move logically to achieve your end—that is, checkmate.

But like most college students, I got my most important lessons outside of the classroom. We had frequent dance parties in Brooklyn's Canarsie section, where I grew up, both in the basements of my friend's homes and in the school gymnasiums. When Tempo City (a former bowling alley turned discotheque) opened a few blocks from my house, the action shifted there. I met a new group of people, including the house band named The Elements. I'd call these guys a garage band, except that their apartments in the projects had no garages. Hanging around with the mostly Jewish musicians from East New York opened a whole new world for me. We danced to the music they played and it was a more intimate, immersive experience. They created the music and we interpreted it. It was softer, more intellectual, easier on the psyche, building up, not breaking down.

So when I took a music course and had questions to which the professor gave pat, unsatisfying answers, I naturally turned to my buddies for information.

Why are there eight natural notes? Why aren't there twelve, or seven, or ten? I asked every one of my musician friends. They had the same reaction as had many of my university professors, and mostly ran away screaming. Finally, I asked a more serious musician friend, composer and pianist Stuart Isacoff. Stu had a very simple answer: it's convention. Some societies use other numbers of notes, and so create different scales. To our Western ear, however, the octave sounds pleasant and natural.

Years later, while watching the Fischer/Spassky match on PBS, I had similar questions about chess. Why do the pieces have to start on those particular squares? Why can't they start at the side of the board, and not the bottom or top? Why can't they start anywhere you want them to start? Where's the creative freedom? This time, however, I had no handy expert to consult. So, questions unanswered, I took myself down to the Marshall Chess Club in Greenwich Village and got me some chess lessons. That's where I first met Bruce Pandolfini—noted author, teacher, and technical chess consultant on various films, most recently for the Netflix hit series *The Queen's Gambit*. Bruce, fresh off his debut as an analyst on Shelby Lyman's PBS coverage of the Fischer/Spassky match, had the answers I sought.

It turns out the answer to the chess piece placement question is very much the same as the eight-note musical question. It's convention. It's how the game was designed and how the patterns work in accordance with the rules. You might place the pieces differently, or even use different pieces, but the game you would be playing wouldn't be chess.

My desire to master chess took off from there, as did my friendship with Bruce. My work career until this point had been the proverbial mixed bag, something I highly recommend to any young person hungry for knowledge and experience. After college, I worked in publishing, copyediting and writing both news and as a critic for Fairchild Publications' *Home Furnishings Daily* and *Women's Wear Daily*. Eventually, I was hired as the Associate Editor at *The Designer*, a monthly magazine for the interior design/architectural industry; I also did a research study at The Fashion Institute of Technology Subsequently, I served as a business consultant, was a women-in-business specialist, and did research on the garment industry for the New York State Department of Commerce. Finally, before striking out on my own, I was the Director of Financed Projects and Director of Public Information for the New York City Industrial Development Agency.

Somewhere in between, my involvement in the chess world led me to work for US Chess Masters, Inc., the first business specifically designed to teach chess to the general public.

It was at this time that I helped Bruce fulfill his first big contract with Simon & Schuster, to produce six chess books. Bruce had founded Chess in the Schools project was then the first Executive Director. Chess in the Schools is a nonprofit organization whose purpose is to bring chess into the public-school classrooms of the underprivileged. They needed instructors. Bruce chose me as one of them. It was a big change for me, but once I started, I never turned back.

During my nine years with Chess in the Schools, I taught in the classroom at four New York City public schools—PS 230, 261, 39, and 321—each classroom as unique and rewarding as the next. By the time I had ended my relationship with Chess in the Schools, I had gained substantial on-the-job training, as well as started down a long and rewarding path that I'm happy to now call a career.

Despite this introduction into my meandering path towards becoming a chess teacher, this book is not a memoir. My story is simply proof that anyone can be a successful instructor for children, particularly at a time when educational innovation is perhaps required. Since we all want the best for children, we should look for new ways to reach them.

I have seen chess bring the most tentative students out of their shells. I have seen students who don't necessarily excel in the classroom exceed in my classroom, and become gifted students. Most importantly, chess—unlike basketball, debate team, even theater—is a game for all, regardless of abilities or aptitudes. It crosses borders, languages, and cultures. The world continues to be fascinated by chess, despite the fact that professional chess is not covered on the nightly news. I think you'd be hard-pressed to find a home today (not just in the states, but internationally) that did not have a chessboard.

Although in this book I mainly discuss my method of teaching chess and critical thinking in afterschool, I hope readers—with a little help and insight drawn from my own experiences in that teaching—can take my advice, modify it, adapt it to their own circumstances, and so advance the vital mandate of educating our children.

PART ONE

Part One of *Strategic Moves* presents exercises and insights to assist in developing critical thinking, problem-solving, and logic.

NEW PEOPLE/OLD PEOPLE OR ASSESSING PERFORMANCE

What's the idea? *In this section, I present the manner in which I probe my new students' level of development and knowledge of the game. A student might be confident, but that doesn't always mean they have the correct knowledge or the ability to present the understanding competently. Discovering the strengths and weaknesses of the new student will be invaluable in the learning experience as the teacher proceeds.*

KIDS FUDGE THE TRUTH. I'M guessing whether you are a parent, a teacher, or simply have spent time around young children, this is no surprise to you. Over the years I've found that only a small percentage of kids who claim to know chess (or geography, or the past ten United States presidents, or how to whip up a shepherd's pie) actually do. And that's why, at the start of a new chess course, I always begin in the same way.

It's the first day of a new course. All of the kids are excitedly bouncing around the classroom. There are a number of new students, whom I barely know beyond their names and grades. A few admit they don't play chess at all. More claim they do. I tell them all that I don't believe them and that they have to prove to me that they do know how to play. Several will become offended at my disbelief. I tell them that everybody must prove they know how to play chess before I allow them to enter the class's general population. That's everybody, no exceptions.

Some new kids regard chess in the same way they would regard a game like chutes and ladders, which can be learned on the go, and naturally they think they can skip the part where I teach moves and rules. To allow them to play causes chaos and lots of arguments. That's why I immediately divide them into two sections. There are the "old people," those who have attended my class before and who I am confident can play according to the rules. I send them over to the chessboards, which are already set at one end of the room. The remainder, the "new people," I send to the rug in front of the demo board (short for "demonstration board," an oversized instructional chessboard that can be hung so it can be seen by a group).

All of the new ones are eager to get started. Although they're supposed to be sitting on the rug and looking at the demo board, they keep turning around, watching the old people playing chess, listening to the friendly banter, and not paying attention to me at the demo board. I have to capture them and get them interested in learning—not an easy task, since some will often overestimate their abilities in order to get to the playing section of the class. Just by asking a few judicious questions, I can easily ferret out those who claim to know how to play, but actually do not, or who have limited knowledge. I ask each of the children who claim to know how to play chess to answer individually:

Who taught you to play?

How does the Queen (or the Rook, or the Knight) move?

What does it mean to be in "check"?

Where do the Rooks go on the board?

If a student gives me an incorrect answer to any of the questions, or response is nothing more than a blank stare, a sputtering "um," or a long rambling non-explanation, I relegate the child posthaste to the new people/no knowledge section. A few have a little knowledge of the game, but after some more prying questions I find they clearly have gaps in their understanding. I ask the new people who say they know how to play to set up the demo board. This will be Test Number One.

Sorting through the class to discover "who knows what" is always fun for me. However, I make sure the kids who don't know the answers to my basic questions feel no shame, by telling them not to worry, that all of us are here to learn. At this point, the new people have been subdivided into two groups: new people/no knowledge, and new people/some knowledge. Along with the old people, this makes for three distinct levels in the room.

By necessity, traditional classroom teachers do not have the time to assess individually the abilities of their new students, as demonstrated in this initial exercise in my classroom. They must play for the majority and meet the relentless schedule set for them by the education system. As an afterschool teacher, though, I'm happy I get to set my own schedule, one which addresses each student, one at a time. Afterschool was a relatively new thing when I began teaching. I like to think I had a hand in shaping the way it subsequently developed, at least in New York City. One thing I discovered right away was that afterschool classes are very different from regular school classes, a fact which, ultimately, led to my love of teaching in enrichment situations.

When I was in grade school, there were no afterschool classes as we understand them today. One day a week I had choir practice with Sister Gemma, with Mr. Nichols on piano, in the lunch room of Holy Family School. On Saturdays I attended dance class at Ex Sisters Dance Studio, where I dabbled in ballet and majored in acrobatics (think gymnastic floor exercises). Afterschool for me meant walking my little brother, James, the half mile home from school. Mom had returned to the working world as soon as James began first grade. It became my job to make sure he did his homework while I did mine. I was responsible for stopping him from burning down the house, or committing any of the myriad little-boy play-damage he and his friends might dream up. I also had to prepare dinner. Little in the way of enrichment courses there, but I did learn. I learned responsibility and got a good dose of reality, which has served me well in adulthood and very likely contributed to my approach as an instructor.

Parents universally want the best for their children: the best economically, the best physically, the best educationally. Ultimately, it's the parents who bear the responsibility for their offspring—regardless if "learning" is done in a proper school. This is trivially true. Perhaps the most important way to meet this responsibility is to ensure that the children have the tools and the training to weigh and evaluate options, so that no matter where they receive their education, in school or in addition to school, they will be prepared to create a functional, happy life.

I feel strongly that my role as a teacher is to develop an educational baseline for instructing children to think critically. Afterschool teachers like me often have years-long relationships with their students, even if they see them only an hour a week. They get to see the children grow in stature and knowledge and mature toward adulthood. There are no report cards: children can develop and learn at their own pace. I get to see the results of my instruction evolve in my students.

But I'm getting ahead of myself. The first step to be taken on this journey to is to establish where the starting point lies. This brings me back to Test Number One: setting up the board.

If you don't know how to play chess, or have been playing informally, this may seem like a nonsensical exercise. It is not. There are strict rules for setting up a chessboard, which I will return to in a later discussion.

The kids on the rug are given an instruction: one person at a time will step up to set up the board. This time they don't believe me and try for a group effort, and if you're thinking this goes quietly, think again. Kids are yelling out answers and interfering. I tell them strongly, "One person at a time," and I choose the order in which they respond. If the new people who say they know how to play the game cannot set it up properly, I immediately doubt they have any real familiarity with chess. So, I quickly shuffle them over to the new people/no knowledge section.

Those kids who demonstrate they can set the board up correctly, including the proper ranks for White and Black, are given Test Number Two: the show-me-how-the-pieces-move phase. I ask them to do this by playing a game with me on the demo board. I make a move for White and ask one of them to make a move for Black. I continue with my second move, followed by a move by another new student, rotating through the group for each successive move. Once again, they're not allowed to help each other, and I tell them clearly that the reason for the game is to determine their readiness, to show me they really do know how to play chess.

Winning isn't necessary, I say; just show me you know how the pieces move. I speak slowly and deliberately and look the kid directly in the eye. Since the kid clearly wants to beat the teacher you might think this statement would cause disappointment. In fact, it does not. Simply proving to me that they do know how to play the game is the big win. Getting out of the new people group and into the old people group is more important to them than beating me.

If they can correctly display how to move the pieces, I ask a few questions:

How do you castle?

What happens when a Pawn reaches the other side of the board?

What is the difference between check and checkmate?

If the new person can correctly describe these two things and tell me precisely what checkmate is (the King is attacked and can't be saved from attack), I then formally dub them old people, and they can join that group to play chess.

I continue to instruct the remaining new people at the demo board.

> **By asking questions and requiring answers, whether demonstrated physically (show me how the pieces move) or verbally (tell me what happens when a Pawn reaches the other side of the board), the student's level of competency can be determined. These kinds of informal tests of knowledge are essential in order to determine how to**

instruct the child, but they do not have to be as stressful as an in-class written quiz. Keep it light and use as much humor as you can manage to squeeze into the session.

After that first session, where I separate the new people into the "knows" and the "don't-knows," then teach the geography of the chessboard to the don't-know people, I introduce a piece or two a week, until, finally, the board is fully set up. I keep each session short, however, in order to allow the students to actually use their hands to play an abbreviated game, using only the pieces they have already learned. This is crucial. The learning cannot be theoretical. It must be put to practical use, and the hand/mind must be connected.

Don't be shy about assessments. Determining where a student is in the process by asking questions and requiring answers is essential, in order to ensure the student is not lost, drowned in the sea of new information. You cannot judge the level of understanding based solely on verbal answers, however, nor can the child fully understand the material until it is realized in action.

Before you can teach a student to add, they must know how to count and they must actually count objects. You must know the notes before you can sing the scales, but the scales are useless until they are actually sung or played. It's the same in teaching children how to play chess.

HOW TO FIND YOUR NAME OR ANALYZATION 101

What's the idea? *This section shows how to present to students a problem to be solved, observe how they go about handling it, and then lead them through the process by the Socratic method. Reading, manual dexterity, and hand/eye coordination are all dealt with here.*

THE YOUNGEST KIDS COME TUMBLING into the classroom where I have been waiting for them, escorted by a young, enthusiastic afterschool minder. Some of the kids already know me from past chess courses and most of them already know each other, being at the same school, within a grade of each other. There is a lot of laughter and positivity in the room, the students flushed with excitement and oodles of energy after a full day of learning. It makes me happy just being there.

At the start of each course, I am provided by the school or program a list of students who have enrolled in my class. Taking attendance is one, if not the only, requirement of the courses I teach. But over the years, I have found ways to turn this seemingly mundane activity into an essential piece of the learning puzzle. It's also the activity in which I learn the names of those new people in my class and put faces to them. For the youngest students (from now forward, when I say youngest, I mean pre-pre-K through kindergarten), it's also my first opportunity to gauge where they are in their learning experience.

I always copy the list of students who have signed up for my class into my own attendance book, one class per page. I want to be able to look at the records and see who has shown up and what dates they studied with me. By now, my file cabinet is overflowing with numerous attendance books with the names of my students and the dates they attended class.

On the first day for my youngest students, the new people and the old people form a line, as they will for each subsequent class. The old people already know what to expect and how to do it. The new people do not. The attendance book is opened to the correct page, their names already written in large block letters. Their assignment is to find their names, follow the line across, and check the correct box under that day's date, which is written on the column above.

Most of the kids find their names without a problem; some do not. I allow these baffled children time to watch the others and to examine the attendance list. This works for a majority of them. For a few, usually the youngest of the young, it does not. They need help, but not answers. I never tell any of them, "Here's your name." Never. That would disempower the learning experience.

It's important to note that it's not necessary for the students to know how to spell their names, just to recognize them when they see them. If, after a long wait, they still can't find their names, I begin to ask questions. I might start by asking them to identify which names have already been checked off, thus eliminating the majority of the list. If this doesn't help, I continue questioning—for example, "What's the first letter of your name? Which of the names on the list have the same first letter?" If that's no help, I persist.

"Is this your name?" I ask, pointing to the first name on the list. If the child says no, I go to the second name, and so on down the list until the child correctly identifies their own name. It's often necessary to repeat this process a few times until the child gets it right. I find patience to be indispensable here. It would be easier for me to show students their own names, but then they wouldn't know how to solve the problem. They would continue to expect someone to solve it for them. Cultivate patience. Sometimes you just have to walk away and let children struggle with a problem themselves. Give them time, and then come back. If you have to help, ask questions. Never give answers.

> **It's worth repeating: patience is a virtue, especially when trying to teach children. I could easily give the child the answer, but that is not a learning**

> **experience. The youngest children may feel overwhelmed when they face a mass of information they haven't been taught to analyze. Simply waiting for the child to find their own name and showing them the logical process to identify the right one ("Is this your name? Let's go one name at a time down the list until we find it.") is of high value in my teaching method. Some things require waiting. If we are impatient for results (such as getting students checked in), we lose the chance to teach logic.**
>
> **Much of what we learn and how we learn it necessitates breaking down a large piece of information into smaller, useful, and digestible bits and then re-assembling them to form a coherent picture, like the pixels in a digital photograph.**

If Tommy or Susie cannot find their own names because they do not know how to spell them, I send them on a research mission: "Check your backpack to see if your name has been written anywhere in it. Maybe mommy or daddy or grandpa wrote it on something, like a book or a jacket or a sandwich." I generally don't find it necessary to camouflage my intent here. I just make sure the children aren't made to feel wrong or small, by assuring them that everything is fine and they're learning, just like the kids sitting in the old people section did in the class last year. I go further, telling them that by next week they'll be able to find their names easily. Support the student as you give instructions and, if possible, inject humor.

If the names have not been found in the backpacks, I check them in and give instructions for them to return next week knowing what their names look like. Very often they return to the next class with their names written on a slip of paper.

Once the students have identified their names, I have an opportunity to teach something that is no longer being taught in school, nor apparently by a large swath of parents at home: how to hold a pencil. Like the signing-in ritual, this may seem trivial, but I think it's one of the most basic lessons on our path to learning. Yes, today's children are writing by hand much less than we did in my day. Keyboard skills are becoming more and more important (and I don't know if typing is being taught either, as it was when I was in high school. As far as I can tell from watching people use a smart device to text, search, or whatever, they use the "hunt and peck" method).

As I hand each of the youngest students the pencil to check themselves in, I observe the way they grasp the pencil. There are many wrong ways to hold a pencil, but only one right one. As soon as I see a child holding the pencil incorrectly, the whole class gets the Pencil Talk. It goes like this:

Human beings are the only animals on the planet that have opposable thumbs. Opposable thumbs means the tip of your thumb can touch the tip of every other finger on your hands. At this point in the talk, I demonstrate what opposable means. As I do so, I watch all the other children, who spontaneously begin to do the same with their fingers. Sometimes a child will ask if monkeys or apes have opposable thumbs, and I inform the class that they do not have fully opposable thumbs. Opposable thumbs allow us to get the "power grip," where the index finger and the thumb grasp an object. Next, I demonstrate the power grip, also called the precision grip. I like to use the word power because it is more meaningful to the students than precision grip. This power grip gives us the most precise hold on any tool, such as pencils, which we use for writing and drawing. It allows us to perform the fine movements necessary for these functions.

Then I make the students hold the pencil properly. From that time on, every time they grasp a pencil in my class, I remind them to hold the pencil properly.

Anything can be turned into an opportunity to instruct or to learn. Be alert for opportunities! The mundane chore of signing in students, of checking off names, doesn't seem likely to provide a learning experience. I have, however,

used it with great effectiveness to evaluate children's skills, to sharpen their physical abilities, and to shape their thinking. In this case, for those youngest students who are mystified by the attendance page and the names on it, I can begin to teach them the logic skills necessary for playing chess or for any problem-solving exercise. I repeat: anything can be turned into an opportunity to instruct, to learn.

Maybe your child already knows how to hold a pencil and may even have mastered the art of clear and articulated name-writing, as well. But generalize these lessons in patience and creative instruction and apply them to various learning situations, from tying a shoe to putting on a winter coat.

After the Pencil Talk, we arrive, finally, at the part where the children get to check the boxes. If the youngest children are baffled by the process, I guide them through it by asking questions.

I show them how to follow across the page with their finger (importantly, they cannot use the pencil to follow across, because they will cross themselves out) until they come to the correct box to check themselves in for the day.

This may be a distance of several inches, depending on the time of year they've entered the program. I show them how to go straight, so they are actually checking themselves in and not the kid above or below them. If we are far across the page, I may suggest they put their initials or some personal mark in their place, so they will be able to find it more easily the next week. As a result, my attendance sheets are usually filled with tiny works of art, and the older the kids get, the more elaborate the mark becomes. You can see how the check-in process may take a long time to complete.

That is precisely why these steps so frequently get skipped in public and private schools. Time is limited in my one-hour-per-week class. The pencil-holding lesson, however, must be learned as early as possible, because the older the child, the more deeply ingrained their method of holding a pencil, until by about second grade it becomes virtually unchangeable.

The experience of finding your name and checking yourself in isn't a root of learning in the same way holding a pencil is. It's different on a basic level. When I teach students how to find their names, I'm really setting the stage for future lessons in research, analyzation, and logic.

Why should I spend half of a class teaching a child to hold a pencil when they don't know the alphabet, though? The answer is simple: holding a pencil is truly foundational. It's the place where we started our evolutionary journey to full humanity. It is essential for toolmaking and use.

Just ask the australopithecines.

THE CHESSBOARD IS NOT A TABLECLOTH OR PATTERN RECOGNITION

What's the idea? *This chapter shows how to give students an opportunity to concentrate on one thing for a sustained period of time, and it is an exercise worth its weight in gold. Practice makes perfect.*

Find ways for your students to ferret out information and articulate what that information is. Continue to mine the data; you never know what will develop. Keep in mind, though, information must be organized to be useful.

WRANGLING A ROOM OF ENERGY-CHARGED kindergartners for a late afternoon chess class is daunting. Half of them are crawling on the floor, doing an imitation of worms (Okay, my fault, as I've taught them an annoying little ditty that has an unfortunate worm as the main and only character). The other half are jumping up and down, singing the ditty and laughing hysterically at the crawlers' antics. Somehow, I have to get them to stand in line to check in, then to sit down to play or to go to the rug for a serious chess lesson. My sleeves are rolled up. I'm ready for the challenge.

The old people are in the far corner, beginning their chess games. My assistant has chosen the color they will play and is supervising them, while I have all the new people sit before a large demo board. (Note: If you are planning to teach a group of children, or even just a single child, I highly recommend investing in one. It saves time and effort and generally makes it easier for children to focus.) Instead of the pieces used on a normal playing board, the demo board pieces are flat and can be inserted into slots at the bottom of the square where you want them to be placed. But to start, we do not use any pieces, just the board itself.

When the students are gathered at the demo board, I ask them if they know what the difference is between a chessboard and a tablecloth. Most will register this question with complete confusion. I can almost hear them thinking: what the heck does a tablecloth have to do with chess? They look at each other with this unspoken question in their eyes.

"The chessboard is *not* like a tablecloth," I say, petting the demo board the same way I would pet a puppy. Then I ask the young ones if they know what a tablecloth is. The same question lingers in their collective eyes, and so I explain that a tablecloth is what grandma puts on the table on Thanksgiving to make it fancy.

I continue, "You just plunk the tablecloth down and set the dishes. A chessboard is not like that. It must be set up in a specific manner. Any other way will not work."

This is my favorite type of teaching moment, the time when the lesson starts to register in the students' minds: the moment it clicks. I've found over the years that this occurs more quickly by presenting analogies.

I continue. "A chessboard is more like a computer. It must be set up in a certain way in order for it to work properly and for us to understand what is happening on it."

I instruct them to look at it—really, really look at it. I make sure that, at least for that moment, all of them are looking at the chessboard. Then I tell them I'm going to leave them to it for a few minutes, and when I come back, I want them to tell me what they see. Then I walk away. I stand behind them and observe.

Most get bored in short order and begin playing with their shoelaces, or gazing out the window, or turning to see what the laughter at the old people's table is all about. If they are very young (pre-pre-K, pre-K, or kindergarten), I will redirect their attention to the board. If they are older, I watch to see where they have diverted their attention. After a short time, I return.

"Who's going to tell me what they see?" I ask.

This is a relatively easy exercise, one that will sharpen children's observational skills and give you a chance to understand their level of perception.

The purpose of this first phase is to assess the ability of the students to concentrate for even a short period of time. Today, the attention span of many children has been severely attenuated, due to the rapid pace of electronic media. But the need to remain focused on one subject at a time is still of high value.

In chess, especially, this is a necessity. One must be able to look at the chess position not only as it is, but also as it might become. Since the chessboard is static and the chess game is dynamic, it's best to begin with what doesn't change and work forward to what does. If you cannot understand what is before you at the moment, you probably have great difficulty imagining a future. Proof of this is the fact that so many college students have no sense of what to study in order to earn a living.

As soon as I ask "What do you see?" one or two hands go up. Sometimes, I will offer a tiny sticker as a reward for answering a question. Many teachers and parents these days hand out rewards for nothing more than batting eyelashes. I do not. A child gets a reward from me only by actually doing something to earn it. But I find this small concession useful to elicit responses from the shyest of the group and to track who has given an answer and who has not. No one gets a second sticker until everyone has a first, and no one is permitted to monopolize the conversation. Each student is allowed to give only one answer until everyone else has had a chance to participate.

"I see squares."

This is generally one of the first answers I get. The chessboard itself is square, a geometric figure that is even on all sides. So if this is the first answer you hear, congratulations—the child is normal.

"Good," I say and sticker them. "How many squares do you see?" The older students will count the squares one by one, by adding lines of squares or by multiplying, according to their math ability. It's usually necessary to inform the youngest that the number of squares is not a mystery. We can determine how many there are by counting, and we proceed to do so as a group.

Then I ask, "What else do you see?" I pick another raised hand and elicit the answer. "Yes, they're green and white." A sticker is awarded. The child beams.

"We don't care what color they are," I say. "We call the lighter squares light and the darker squares dark, no matter what color they are." Then I point out the various colors of squares on the boards in the classroom. Which one is light, the red or the white?

I continue: "What else do you see?"

Once upon a time, a little girl I will never forget raised her hand with enthusiasm. When I called on her, she excitedly announced she saw flowers. Since I had never heard that response before, I asked her to show me the flowers, and she came up to the demo board and pointed to a1, a3, b2, c1, and c3, four dark squares she interpreted as petals with a center. Then she continued to show me other flowers all over the board. Brilliant!

Most often, though, the bravest student in the class, probably one who has already claimed to know how to play chess, ventures, “I see letters and numbers.” Answered and stickered. I keep asking students, in rotation: which letters (another answer, another sticker), which numbers (sticker), how many letters (sticker), are there as many letters as there are numbers (sticker)….

> **It’s always interesting to me that the most obvious characteristic of the chessboard is rarely brought up early in the discussion: that the colors of the squares alternate from light to dark. More often someone will tell me that there are slots at the bottom of the squares before anyone mentions the alternation of color. I usually have to probe deeply to elicit that information. I must ask, “Is there a pattern that you see?”**
>
> **How many times do we miss the obvious, ignore the blatant, miss the forest for the trees? Do we get lost in the**

minutia and take the big picture for granted? Always look for the overall first, then see how the individual fits in and relates.

After we discuss the alternation of colors, I ask if there are any lines of squares that have the same color, and the class learns about the diagonals.

One of my favorite tricks is to point out a two-square dark diagonal, and follow by asking someone to point out a four-square light diagonal, and then I ask them to show me the nine-square dark diagonal. This is a trick, because there is no nine-square diagonal. I let them wrestle with this conundrum for quite a while until one of them finally announces there is no nine-square diagonal and tells me why.

Now it is time to get to the heart of the matter: learning the language of chess, algebraic notation, and the reason for the letters and numbers on any instructional chessboard.

The files run between players and have letter names: a-file, b-file, and so on. (Please see diagram below.) The ranks have number names: 1st rank, 2nd rank, and so on, and run across the board in front of the player. By combining the letter and number, we get a name for every square, and every square establishes its own identity. Again: the chessboard is not a tablecloth.

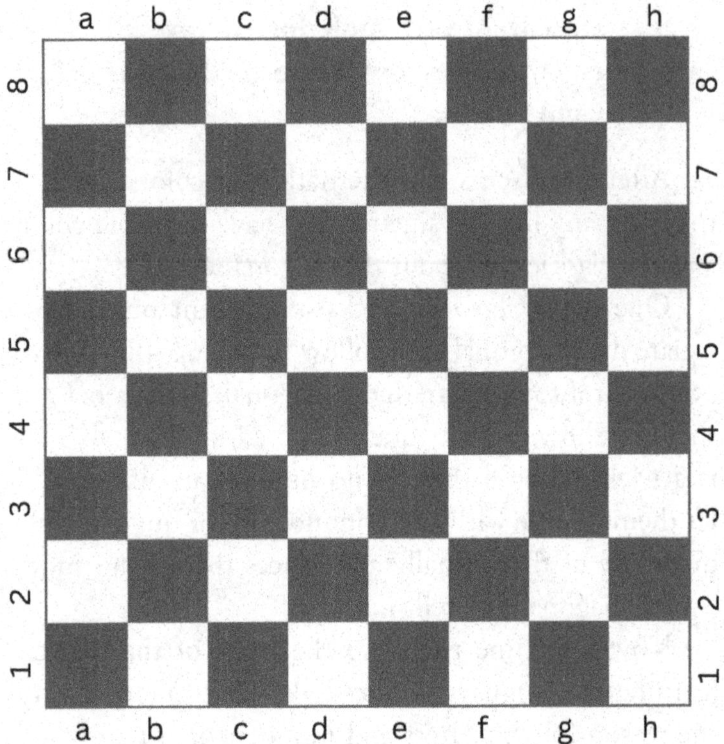

I stress as clearly and directly as possible that the White pieces *always* begin the game on the 1st and 2nd ranks and the Black pieces always start on the 7th and 8th. *Always.* To place the pieces randomly (as I wanted to do before I took myself to the Marshall Chess Club for instruction), or to place the pieces on the files instead of the ranks, violates chess law, and I won't have it. No matter how experienced students are, if I ever find them playing a game with the pieces set up incorrectly, I push all of them to the center of the board, tell them the game doesn't count because the board was set up incorrectly, and make them start over.

After I teach something important, like placement of the White and Black pieces on the board, I frequently ask, "What did I just say?" If no one volunteers to answer the question, I choose a student to do so. If the child gives me an incomplete answer, I say, "That's correct, but it's not complete," and I solicit further information. If the answer is incorrect, I say, loudly and distinctly, "NO," proceed to give the correct reiteration, and ask again what I said. I continue to do this until I am sure I am understood.

This lesson generally marks the end of the day's teaching for the youngest. It's now time to test what the new people have learned in practicality by making their own chessboards.

> **In order to operate in any milieu, you must have a good working knowledge of the terrain. The ranks, files, and diagonals of the chessboard are the highways of play. They organize the thought process and give us a way to discuss the game. In the same way, to do long division you must know how to multiply. To write a symphony you must know musical notation. To do chess you must know the names of the squares, and you must have a language to describe what it is you are doing,**

or will do, or have done. If you don't have this grounding, you won't know how to interpret the present or project the future.

Moreover, squares have meanings to the chess player. a1 is where the Queen's Rook starts the game. e4 is the first move for a King's Pawn opening. Successful opening and endgame patterns are well known because they have been researched through play across the millenia and because we have them written down, we can analyze the results. This gives different squares and different patterns of piece movement a depth of meaning. This knowledge and understanding can be used to solve problems

MAKE YOUR OWN CHESSBOARD OR PUTTING THE LESSON INTO ACTION

What's the idea? *You want to be able to gauge the abilities of students to absorb what has been taught, to analyze new iterations of that knowledge, and to translate it into what they have just learned. You also want to judge their hand/eye coordination. This chapter tells you how I do it.*

I LEAVE THE DOOR TO MY classroom open for a variety of reasons, the most important of which is to ensure transparency. But one unfortunate result is that my noisy charges can be heard all up and down the halls. It's not surprising other teachers on the floor come into my room to see if everything is okay, and occasionally to ask for a quieter atmosphere. Although I am very strict about some behavior (language and violence, for example), noise generally doesn't bother me. You see, except when I am teaching moves and rules to the new people, I do not give lectures. First of all, you can't get the kids to sit still and listen to a long (or even a short) talk in an afterschool setting. They are in chess class to kill each other on the chessboard, and they want to get to it as soon as possible. There's no sense in fighting that reality. Additionally, I find it much more effective to do my instruction almost entirely on an individual basis. I walk around the room and observe the games in progress. I see an issue or an opportunity, stop and give instruction, then proceed to the next board.

Most afterschool classes run for an hour. For the youngest students, this is a very long time—too long, in fact, so for them I stop the teaching and the games at about the forty- to forty-five-minute mark. That's enough for the little kids at one time, and although they may not be ready for the class to end, they are ready for a change of pace. For this reason, I reserve the last fifteen to twenty minutes of those classes for activities at the art table. I call it the art table, but actually it's just two smaller tables pushed together where we gather as a group to do mazes, or to make posters and chessboards.

In all of my classes, the boards and pieces are already set up when the students arrive. For this one reason alone, having an assistant for classes of more than six students is very nearly indispensable; but even if I am on my own, this is a practice I have found to be an absolute non-negotiable. While I'm gathering the students and getting them checked in, the prepped boards are all ready for immediate use. Most of my classes have between fifteen to twenty-five students, though classes with the youngest generally have fewer. If the class arrives without the boards set up, chaos erupts, and you end up squandering a good ten or fifteen minutes of valuable class time. The same principle is applicable at the end of the day, when the equipment must be neatly stowed for the next class.

This is tremendously important because afterschool classes, like normal classes, have fixed endings. There are time constraints. You either cover the intended material, or you do not. Parents or caretakers will be there to pick up the kids, and I can assure you they don't like waiting. Goodness knows the end of my class is not the end of the day's activities for either the kids or their parents. A fresh load of tasks and busyness awaits at home.

Not only is the time for each class predetermined, but the number of classes for each term is also set out and cannot be increased or decreased. I've been told many times by various afterschool coordinators that it doesn't matter if all the children learn how to play a complete game of chess by the end of the term. I disagree. It does matter to me. I was hired to teach the children to play chess, and I will do my utmost to ensure that all of them do learn it, and learn it well before the semester ends, so they will have time to play complete games before Parents' Visitation Day arrives.

At the end of the last class of the day, the students are mandated to reset the board with pieces and put one set into an individual set bag. The individual bags are then gathered together and put into the large tote where we keep all the equipment for the class. The last class of the day is generally composed of the school's oldest children. I require them to carry the bags down to the school office, where the sets are stored until the next week. Because I'm scrupulously careful about the materials necessary to run the class, we do not have to replace them often, which can become expensive.

Traditional classroom teachers are given scant funds for relatively essential classroom needs, like pens and other materials. Afterschool classes get even less. If you are a parent, you know how quickly things find their way into the Land of the Lost and need to be replaced, only to reappear once a replacement has been procured. Show respect for teaching materials, preserve them with care, and do as much as you can to impart to your child how necessary this is.

Just as important, at the end of any game played, insist that the child reset the pieces. This means the set will be ready at the beginning of the next game or class, and the number of pieces lost through carelessness is minimized. Otherwise, you are guaranteed (particularly if you have a younger child) to find a lonely Rook or Bishop under the couch, in the dog's mouth, or buried in the backyard.

This frequently happens in my classrooms, too. At the end of nearly every game, someone can't find a Bishop or a Knight, and I respond to the complaint by pointing out that the chess pieces don't have feet, so if they were there during the game, they are there now.

Showing respect for the class materials shows respect for the teacher and for the providers of those materials. Things do not just appear spontaneously and get replaced if they are trashed. General respect for material things as well as for people has diminished in recent years. This is not good for the learning process or for our larger society. Making the kids feel a sense of responsibility by assigning them a specific responsibility for some part of the functioning of the class helps them take more seriously what happens there. Our actions have consequences, and the sooner children learn this lesson, the easier it will be for them to succeed in life.

After the old people have reset their chessboards, the youngest students are called to the art table. The new people are handed a blank, eight-by-eight grid, with letters (a through h) and numbers (1 through 8) flanking on all sides. I make the blank grid myself using graph paper and copy it before class. It's important to make several more copies than the number of new students in the class, as we can expect at least one to get ruined in the process of creating the individual chessboards.

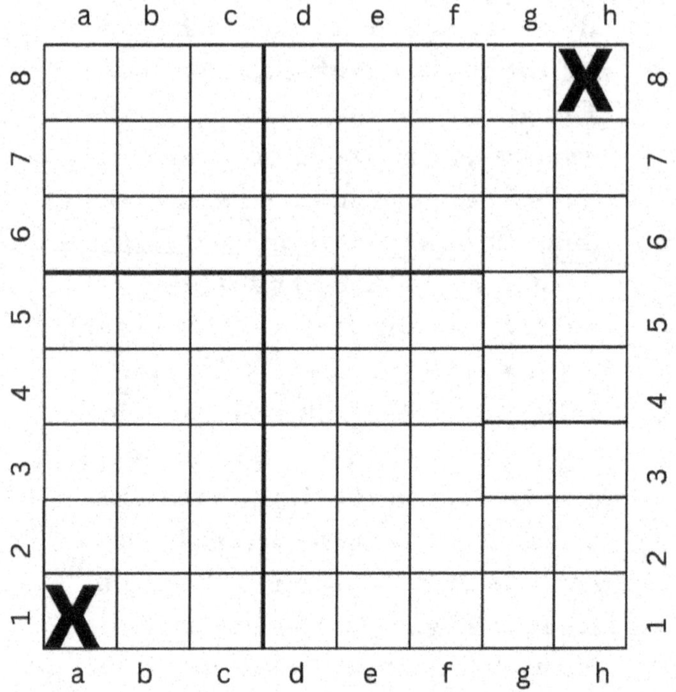

On squares a1 and h8, which are dark squares in opposite corners of the board, I draw great big Xs. The kids are instructed to draw an X in every dark square. The demo board is left out on display as a reference. This isn't an exercise in memory. I allow, indeed sometimes encourage the kids to look at the demo board in order to successfully complete the task.

I find it fascinating to observe the various methods the kids use to approach this assignment. In most of today's classrooms, the children sit at communal tables (like the art table) facing each other, rather than in straight rows of desks facing the teacher, as they did when I was at school. This single fact has great impact on the way in which children are learning. They are instructing each other nearly as much as the teacher is instructing them. Learning, in some schools, has become a cooperative affair. It encourages constant discussion between peers—and inevitably, not all the talk is likely to be about the subject at hand.

The efficacy of the new learning philosophy can be, and surely is, debated; but one thing is sure: playing chess is not a communal affair. In fact, it is a highly individualized endeavor. Yes, there are variants, such as "bughouse chess," a team-chess variant the kids love, where four to six people play the game at once. Such options are more cooperative than standard chess, but the students play the standard game most of the time, and this book is about the standard. Besides, it serves each child well in life to learn to succeed on one's own. Perhaps you don't know just how much children are collaborating in school and on homework these days. Take this opportunity to teach the child to think for him or herself.

At the schools where I've taught, sitting at group tables instead of stand-alone desks is nearly universal in all pre-K and kindergarten classes, and assisting the children to perform tasks is generally accepted, even by myself. However, in my chess class the students are not only encouraged to work independently: I require it.

> **Individual responsibility is a good thing to teach children. It's the best way for them to grow and learn and its effects spread across all facets of learning. After spending the time to analyze the data of chessboard geometry, an opportunity should be provided for each student to put the information to use. Since there is nothing mysterious about the alternating colors of chessboard squares, the problem of replicating the pattern should be solved easily. There is nothing difficult about placing an X in a box. Even preschoolers should be able to do it. Fingers must learn to do what the brain orders, and this is their first opportunity to practice it. They learn hand/eye coordination and the attention to detail needed to successfully complete the task. This exercise is the first step in establishing the pattern for all learning in the future.**

Each student will display different approaches to solving the create-your-own-chessboard exercise, a fact which I find fascinating. One method I often see is the child filling the diagonal that runs from a1 to h8 with Xs.

Diagonals are the last thing I taught them, and that may account for the frequency with which students use it. It's correct as far as it goes, but many falter after filling in that first diagonal and often get lost. They need to be reminded of the alternating pattern and start at a1, working to complete the a-file before going on to the b-file, or before continuing with the dark diagonal that runs from a3 to f8.

Other kids start at a1 and logically work their way up the a-file without any coaching. This is the most productive method, even if they sometimes make mistakes and put two Xs in a row. If this is the case, I ask them to identify the mistakes they have made and we fix them together.

A few children just start putting X randomly in the squares. They need the most teaching to complete the assignment, and they are also the ones who may need to have the blank grid replaced.

Again, I don't give any answers. The answers are already there for discovery, as long as the student searches for them. For the first group, those using the diagonal method, I redirect them to a1. For those who use the second method—beginning at a1 and working logically up the a-file—but who may have made mistakes, I ask them to identify the place where they went wrong, and then I erase the error. This is an important foundational exercise. Identifying the error point and correcting it lays the groundwork for planning ahead.

For the last group of students—those who have no clear method of solving the problem—I erase the errors or provide a new grid. Then we begin at a1, where I have pre-provided a large, hand-drawn X.

"This one has an X. Is it light or dark?" I ask. Then we go to a2, and I continue: "a1 is dark and there's an X in it. Is a2 light or dark? Do we put an X in it or not?"

I continue up the a-file, asking the same questions for each square, and continue to the b-file at b8—the square adjacent to a8, which is a light square.

"This square is light," I say, pointing to a8. "We didn't put an X in it. What color is this square?" I point to b8. "Do we put an X in it or not?"

I've described this process in what may seem to be excruciating detail for a good reason: so that parents or other non-traditional teachers have a model to follow in their own educational efforts. This method of asking questions instead of giving answers teaches the students how to work logically to solve the problem at hand—in this case, making their own chessboards. The repetition of the questions from one square to the next reinforces the lesson over and over again.

The result is that the student learns to take one step at a time and connect the

> **results both to what has gone before and what will come after. This is the heart of logic: *if this, then that.***

Chess, as you might expect, can be argued as a game of logic. If I put my Pawn here, then my opponent's Queen will snatch it. Then I will do this, my opponent will do that, and so forth. Logic. Strategies and tactics come through logical thinking, but cannot be nurtured by lectures or reading alone. The student must actually play the game, move the pieces, see the results of their actions. Many times, I make the analogy to riding a bicycle. I can tell you how to do it, but until you put your feet on the pedals and push, you're not riding.

WHAT IS A QUESTION? OR DEVELOPING DATA

What's the idea? *This chapter shows how to instruct the child on the difference between what one thinks or feels, and what the hard facts of the matter are.*

"DOES ANYONE HAVE ANY QUESTIONS?"

You've heard teachers ask this before, and of course when I say this at the end of a lesson, I mean questions about the material I've just presented. But as you might expect, not everyone interprets it that way. A little boy I'll call Mr. Striped Shirt raises a hand. (When I don't know a student's name, I use an unmistakable nickname. In this case I choose the pattern of his shirt, a yellow-and-blue long-sleeved tee.) I give him a nod and he stands, perhaps with a finger in his nose or a grubby scratch to his chest as he does it. Striped Shirt begins a long-winded recitation, garbled and rambling, about his father and grandfather. I cannot see a point to this tale and interrupt.

"Excuse me, Mr. Striped Shirt, but what is your question?"

He stares at me for a moment, blinking. Then I continue:

"Do you know what a question is?"

No one in the group answers. Not one of the pre-Ks and kindergartners know what a question is. Not one. Interestingly, this is not unusual. The first time it happened, I was surprised. The second time, I was shocked. By the third, fifth, fiftieth times, I understood no one had ever taught them about questions. That's odd, I thought. With my own background, I found it hard to imagine. Yet I knew the kids asked questions all the time.

"Can I have another cookie?" for example.

"Can I go to the bathroom?" is another good one.

So, I have to stop the chess instruction and give a talk on questions.

"Ms. Carol," I say, channeling the high-pitched voice of a kindergartner. They giggle at my imitation. "Can you please tell me again which ones are the ranks and which are the files?" I pause and look around at their sweet little faces. At this point they are blank. I know I haven't gone far enough.

"When you don't understand something the teacher says, you ask for more information." Then I ask again: "Does anyone have a question?" No one ever raises a hand. I'm not sure anyone got the point, so I have to go further.

"This is the teaching part of the class," I tell them. "We only have a little time to get this part done, or you won't have time to play chess. Right now, if you don't understand something I say, you raise your hand and ask a question. Later we tell stories. Got it?"

Everyone nods dutifully, but no one asks a question.

> **As an instructor, I firmly believe it's important to know when to ask a question, but it's more important to know what question to ask and how to ask it. You have to know what information your students are missing. You may have inadvertently left out data, or assumed your students already had the knowledge to interpret correctly what you said, or expressed the information inadequately.**
>
> **Alternatively, the students may have become engrossed in one idea being presented and missed an important point, or may have gaps in their data set that made what was being presented unintelligible, or may have an entirely different perspective that needs to be explored in context.**
>
> **Each of these possibilities requires a different type of question and a different tone. Careful phrasing and presentation make asking the hard question easy.**

Most teaching of this nature takes place in the early days of each course and is addressed to the new students. The old students have already heard my lectures on these matters and are applying or not applying my instruction in varying degrees. To be fair, some things are more important than others to the students' success in playing chess (or in life, for that matter).

There is one thing, though, that is of paramount importance when teaching beginners.

I'm sitting at the demo board surrounded by new students. We've been playing a game, with me taking the White pieces and they taking turns moving for Black. It's Mr. Orange Pants's turn to go, and I ask:

"What's your move?"

Mr. Orange Pants responds, "Well, maybe—"

I stop him right there. Maybe is not a good way to proceed in chess. "There are no *maybes* in chess," I tell him. "In chess, we figure it out. It's like math. We figure it out."

"But," Mr. Orange Pants might continue, "I feel like—"

Again, I stop him. "In chess, we don't *feel* like anything. In chess, we figure it out," I repeat, this time with more emphasis. "In math, do we say, 'I feel like two plus two equals seventeen'? No! We figure it out."

Now I'm in full dramatic mode and continue with the analogy, two fingers on each hand held aloft. "But I really feel like two plus two is seventeen. Really. That's what I *feel!*" I clasp my hands, clutch my chest, and feign pleading.

Now I change my tone, reverting to the teacher. "Just because I really feel like two plus two is seventeen, it doesn't make it so, does it? No, it does not! In math we figure it out." I again hold up two fingers on my left hand followed by two fingers on my right hand and count it out—one, two, three, four.

"It doesn't matter what I feel, two plus two is always four. I can figure it out, and what I feel has nothing to do with it. It's the same thing in chess. We figure it out. We use logic. We use our brains.

"Do you know what logic is?" I ask. One kid may respond jokingly that logic means you figure it out, but that thinking just goes around in a circle, so I have to explain further.

"Logic means that if *this* happens, then *that* follows. If you take this protected Pawn, for example, then I will take back. If you take and then I take, it's even. If I don't take back, then *whoopee!* You're ahead a Pawn.

"In chess, we go through the 'what ifs' and the responses to them, and then we pick the best option for ourselves. What happens if I move my Rook here? Can it be captured? What happens if I attack the Queen with my Rook? Where will the Queen move to get away? This is what you think when it's your turn to move. What happens if my opponent attacks my Bishop? Is my Bishop defended? Is it an even trade? Can I block the attack? What happens if my opponent takes my Knight? Is it defended? Can I take back safely? That's what you think when it's your opponent's turn to move."

Sometimes I can see the light go on in a student's brain as I go further into the meaning of figuring it out using logic.

> **In life we often get our emotions involved in areas where logic should reign. We should always be questioning how events will proceed if one decision is made over another. Logic can really help us here, but it's not the only place. It's just an easy example.**

Be careful what you ask for, or what you teach, for that matter. Once they've learned logic, they'll use it against you.

As I've already said, noisy classrooms don't bother me, but inappropriate language does. I learned early on that I had to institute strict (and I mean strictly enforced) rules concerning what words are allowed in my classroom. I have more than a few of these taboos, but even for the youngest (perhaps especially for the youngest) I clearly announce the following:

> *"No body parts.*
> *"No bodily functions."*

You might incorrectly think that a kindergartner would not understand these dictums. You would be wrong. They understand them very well. Almost immediately a hand goes up.

"Ms. Carol?" Mr. Green Shirt asks with a sly smile. "Can we say 'hand'? A hand is a body part."

He uses hand as an example because I frequently tell them to think with their brains, not with their hands, so he knows he's got me there. Logic personified.

MAZES AND MISTAKES OR ANALYSIS IN ACTION

What's the idea? *This section shows how to give your students the opportunity to make mistakes, to learn from them, and to develop the skill to identify and rectify them. It builds upon lessons previously taught and furthers the students' skills in collecting information and putting it to practical use.*

FOR MY YOUNGEST STUDENTS, MY chess classes end at the art table to do mazes (except for new people's first class, where they do the make-your-own-chessboard exercise). The less-experienced students are given very simple mazes. The more experienced the student is, the more complicated the mazes become. The children love this part of the class. We sit around a common table, talk, make jokes, and laugh.

I have a huge assortment of mazes for just these occasions. I take the appropriate mazes to the class, copy them at the school, and hand out specifically chosen mazes, just one per person to specific children. It's important to note that I do not dump a pile of mazes on the table, because then the kids will not treat the exercise seriously, but will make mistakes, toss the errors, and take a fresh maze. The idea is to teach them how to problem-solve.

I also come equipped with a box full of pencils for the kids to use. However, these are not just any pencils—no, no, no! Just as with the mazes, they, too, are purposefully chosen.

No child is allowed to grab a marker or crayon from the classroom, for any reason. I do not allow the children to do mazes or make chessboards with any writing instrument that is permanent. When we do the "make your own chessboard" exercise or solve mazes, I supply the pencils. This is one of my favorite teaching tricks.

What is so special about a box of pencils you may ask? Well, I'll tell you. Most of the pencils in the box are short and stubby, though a few of the pencils are tall. Some have pretty colors, or have designs pleasing to kiddie eyes, like stars or baseballs or stylized animals or a sparkly finish. A few are your standard yellow. None of them, however—not one—has an eraser. Every possible eraser has been worn down or has tragically broken off. But sitting in the box among these random and haggard pencils is a big pink eraser, and I am the only one who is allowed to touch it. It's mine.

Again, this is purposeful and in furtherance of the objective: to teach problem-solving. When a mistake happens, we do not give up.

At some point, the inevitable happens. Someone makes a mistake, and a hand shoots up in the air. That's when the class gets my Everybody Makes Mistakes talk. It goes like this:

Everybody makes mistakes. Everybody. I make mistakes all the time, but when a mistake happens, we have to fix it. If you make a mistake, bring it to me and we'll fix it.

Again, this is purposeful. At this stage of the problem-solving education, you want to see what mistakes are being made and how good the students are at recognizing where they went wrong. This method lays the foundation for much of what chess teaches.

> **There will be innumerable instances of irreparable mistakes in life. There's nothing we can do about them, but in the future try to avoid them in the first place. When an error can be fixed, learning to recognize and repair it is a life skill worth having. Even if the mistake you make cannot be fixed (like filling every avenue in a maze), you can learn from it. You can prevent something like it from happening again, or know what to do when faced with a similar situation. Recognizing and admitting the difference between an error and bad luck is crucial to this process.**
>
> **Too often we attribute an error to bad luck instead of to our own fallibility. We see the propensity to err as a source of shame, as a weakness instead of an opportunity to learn; and in so doing**

we limit our chance to learn and grow. When you make a mistake, admit it, fix it, and move on.

Some new students do not hear my instructions the first time. If they don't, however, they'll certainly hear them when I catch them working on a maze where every possible avenue has been filled in with pencil lines, doubled over, with lines crossing over barriers—and then tell me they're done. Everybody-makes-mistakes talk redux. New copy of maze. Do over.

If an old person makes a mistake, they know what to do. They raise their hand and say:

"Ms. Carol, I made a mistake."

I ask them to show me the error, and after they point it out, I ask them how far back they need me to erase. They analyze their work and show me the error point. I then thoroughly erase from that point forward, and they continue on their way. It doesn't matter how many times the children make a mistake on any one maze. They show it to me and identify the error point. I erase and they continue.

If Mr. Gray Shoes is making too many mistakes in a maze, I teach him how to avoid going astray. Don't start by moving the pencil, I say. Begin with your finger, just like we did when you signed into the attendance book and had to follow your name's row across the page to the correct date column. In the maze, use your finger to trace a path for a short distance, then go back and fill in the line with pencil. Repeat until the maze is complete.

As your charge is learning chess, I suggest doing this maze exercise at the start or the end of each class. Through years of teaching, I have learned that repetition with growing complexity is the most effective way to shape the mind's pathways.

> **Errors in making chessboards or doing mazes are all fixable. Identifying the mistake, however, is a skill that must be taught and learned. I am always pleased by how little effort it takes to get my students to identify the error made and how well they adapt to the procedure. Each time they do, they deepen their brain's pathways in a method of problem-solving.**

This same process of problem-solving happens during chess games, particularly when a newer student is playing a more experienced player, or when two newer players face each other. This often happens in the classes where I'm working with older, more experienced players. When two newer players face each other, I frequently hear the words, "You're cheating!" yelled out.

That word, cheating, is not allowed in my class. It's inflammatory. It provokes fights. We don't use it. When I hear it, my response is immediate. I inform the offender that we don't use that word, but instead of saying cheat, we should say: "Ms. Carol, I think my opponent made a mistake."

Since the rest of the class already know this phrase and know it well, they echo it. Within seconds, everyone is mimicking me, and I hear, "Ms. Carol, I think my opponent made a mistake," erupt all around me. The accuser gets the point quickly. This is a firm class rule and violations will not be tolerated.

As soon as the chorus of "Ms. Carol, I think my opponent made a mistake" calms down, I ask the accuser to tell me what happened. I tell them not to touch the pieces—that if they do touch the pieces, or make a move of any kind, I will not be able to find out what went wrong. I expect to be told exactly and in detail what happened.

There are several reasons disputes of this kind occur. With the youngest students, they are often testing their opponents and the rules of the game. Can I alter the rules? Ignore the rules? Does my opponent know the rules well enough to call me out if I violate them? When they have been playing chess at home with a parent (likely a father playing his son) who is breaking rules to keep the game friendly and to boost the child's ego, mistakes are more likely to be tolerated.

Among those older children who have a good grasp on the rules and know better than to try to fool their opponents, it's different. Generally, it is a true mistake of some sort. Maybe someone has moved twice in a row, without realizing their opponent has yet to make a move. Perhaps they have made a hand/eye coordination error and accidently placed a light-squared Bishop on a dark square.

To solve the mystery, I usually ask the accuser to tell me what happened in words—not by picking up and moving any pieces. I require the opponent to be silent and tell them they'll have their chance to tell their side of the story next, and they do. After I see both sides of the disagreement, I can make a decision. For example, if someone has moved twice, or misplaced a Bishop, it becomes apparent. We fix the mistake and the game continues.

If we cannot identify the error, I might suggest ending the game and beginning another, or offer the alternative of flipping a coin. The players choose.

Mistakes happen, just like differences of opinion happen. Inflammatory language never helps resolve the problem, it just provokes fights and bad feelings. Both sides must be heard in a calm, dispassionate manner. This is the only way we can learn and grow.

Moreover, each time the student repeats the process of retracing past actions, analyzing them, identifying error points, and fixing the mistakes, the method becomes more deeply ingrained and eventually becomes natural.

PARTNER VS. OPPONENT OR COMPETITION

What's the idea? *The ability to distinguish between someone you work with to accomplish a goal (a partner) and someone who is trying to win (an opponent) is vital for any success. Examples of how to proceed in so doing are given in this chapter. Additionally, the talent of coping with an opponent without accompanying rancor is discussed.*

THERE WILL BE TIMES IN your teaching or parenting journey in which you'll need a little bit of help when it comes to instruction. Much of this book is about providing you with the toolkit to do this effectively. This process also applies to how you instruct others to teach, whether it's a husband or wife, a babysitter, or any number of caregivers, tutors, and coaches you might encounter.

For years, I've often brought in a former student or other chess player to become an assistant in my afterschool classes. On occasions, I've needed more than one helper, especially when the number of students in the class is more than twenty. For example, at The Berkeley Carroll School, where Bruce and I have taught since 1993, we frequently have thirty or more students. In most cases, Bruce takes one classroom with the older, more advanced and experienced students, and I take another classroom with the new people and younger students. The school has provided us with an assistant (sometimes two assistants) for many years.

As I mentioned earlier, assistants have a key role in the classroom. Before class begins, the assistants bring the boards and sets to the classrooms and have them ready when the children enter, in order to avoid chaos and get everyone settled down to learn and play the game. I insist the chessboards be set up properly and loaded into individual chess bags after each game and at the end of each class. If they have not been, we can waste another ten minutes while the kids search around for all their pieces.

> **Like the Boy Scout motto, *Be Prepared!* Know what you want to accomplish and have at hand any materials necessary to do so. Thinking things through in advance makes the road to success easier.**

Assistants are also needed to keep track of students who leave the room to use the bathroom, because only one at a time is permitted to go. If I know and trust the assistant, I allow them to play chess with the students, but I caution them not to give instruction unless I know them very well. This might seem a little severe, but misinformation is more damaging to the overall operation of the class than no information. That's how misunderstandings and arguments start.

If we are not clear on the rules, whether in chess or in the operation of civil society, the resulting confusion can cause discord. Discord is different from healthy debate, in that it's rancorous and leads to bad feelings.

Assistants are also charged with keeping order in the room by quieting particularly raucous kids. If you think a chess class is comprised of kids sitting and contemplating their next moves, think again. Chess classes are loud, often so loud that teachers from other classes come in to see what all the noise is about. It's not that the kids are arguing (I settle all arguments)—it's that the competitive spirit needed to play chess frequently manifests itself physically. But this physicality is not belligerent. My students often sing or dance. Any sort of nonviolent release is fine. While I am very strict about certain rules, in some ways I am very lenient. I do not care about the level of friendly noise until it hits jet-plane levels, and even then I just bring it down to below subway-train levels, so I can be heard without screaming.

When I have a new assistant—one assigned by the school or afterschool program, and not one I've recruited—I have several teaching opportunities. The opportunities I'm writing about here are not opportunities for the students, but for the assistant, who is used to working in afterschool classes for art or acting or robot-building, or in rooms where homework is being done. Things are done differently in my afterschool chess classes, and the new assignee must learn my methods, methods I've developed through experiment and experience across the years.

They must be trained to operate according to my principles, and I have to do so without making anyone feel inadequate or embarrassed, because I want to keep the assistant engaged and learning so they can continue to grow and learn. A little humor helps accomplish this.

> **I have many difficult lessons to teach in chess, and—as a female trying to teach aggressive little boys—if I don't want to be steamrolled, it's mandatory to take a strong stand on tough issues. If that's the only way the kids perceived me, though, the number of students would dwindle, not grow. To do the tough teaching and keep everybody happy, I've found a little humor goes a long way, and I think this applies across the board in all leadership situations.**

When it comes time for the students to start playing a chess game, the new assistant often says, "Sit at the table with your partner."

I cannot let this pass uncommented, and so I interrupt:

"We do not have partners in chess!"

After the new assistant stops dead in their tracks and turns to stare at me, I go on to explain.

"A partner is someone you cooperate with to achieve an end." This statement is accompanied with a gesture with my fingers intertwined and wiggling joyfully, as if to show my left hand working together with my right hand.

"In chess we have opponents." This statement is accompanied by a gesture of my two fists tapping each other head on, like rams in mating season.

"An opponent is someone who is trying to win. In chess we have opponents." Then I repeat: "In chess we do not have partners. (Fingers wiggle.) In chess we have opponents. An opponent is someone who is trying to win." (Rams headbutt.)

> **The amusing gestures take the pressure off the strong statement, as does singing an old or silly song, or making a funny face. Just make sure that the people you're addressing do not mistake the humor for a lack of seriousness concerning the directions given.**

Students are permitted to choose their own opponents only on special occasions, like Parents' Day. I do the choosing, or the kids will inevitably pick either a friend (in which case little real chess-gaming is done) or someone they think they can beat. You'd be surprised how quickly they can sort themselves out.

I have many light but interesting ways of manipulating the pairings. For example, in the youngest classes, I give everyone a three-by-four-inch slip of paper and tell them to write their names on it. If we have more than one child with the same name, a last initial must be included. I then take half the names and put them in a chess bag (these are the "pickees", and they get the White pieces), and I call the others (the "pickers," who get the Black pieces) to draw a name out of the bag as an opponent.

The process is not as random as it appears, because if I don't want certain people to play each other, I either keep both their names in the bag or both out of it.

For the youngest, another method I have for selecting opponents is the same-color method. I ask everyone with a certain color shirt, or socks, or shoes to step forward, and I pair them seemingly randomly. Sometimes we do a version of musical chairs, where I first arrange the kids in size order, then sing something like "Oh! Susannah" or "She'll Be Coming 'Round the Mountain" for a minute, and when I stop, they sit at the first available board. This method also negates the need to choose color.

For the older students, I use more complicated systems. For example, I may ask them to add the numbers in their mothers' (or mothers' surrogates') phone numbers until they get one digit, and then pair them from there. Even more devious, I ask them to translate their first names into numbers (A = 1) and then add them. Students with the same first name include the first letter of their last name.

Opponents pop up sometimes unexpectedly, and we must be ready to meet our opposition wherever it stands.

NEVER BELIEVE YOUR OPPONENT OR NEVER BELIEVE YOUR OPPONENT

What's the idea? *Your opponent is trying to win. Here I show how to reinforce the ability to recognize and analyze data, regardless of its source, and to introduce the necessity of independent thought.*

BEFORE YOU CAN PLAY THE game of chess, you must learn all the rules and moves. This, for the youngest students, will take as many as six classes to accomplish. Remember: You must introduce the pieces slowly and give the kids a chance to play the game each week.

On week one, they get only Pawns. Pawns are the hardest piece to learn because they move differently from how they capture, and they can never move backward, only forward.

On week two, I introduce Rooks. I may also give them Bishops on week two, if I feel the class is capable of it. Both Rooks and Bishops are very easy to learn. Now the kids are playing with Pawns, Rooks, and Bishops. This allows me to introduce the basics of chess opening—that is, don't move too many Pawns. Try to move just the center Pawns and take the other pieces out through the door you've created. Most of the new kids want to move all their Pawns, since they are most familiar with them. So, I tell them the "Walls of the House" story. It goes like this:

Have you ever gone on vacation? The class nods, and perhaps someone calls out about where they went. When you go on vacation, do you lock all the doors and windows, or do you leave them all open? They tell me they lock the doors. Do you leave all the doors and windows open and call out, "Hey burglars! Come on in! We have a really big TV in here. Mom's jewelry is in the bedroom! I have an Xbox! Come on in and get them!"

Of course, they agree that leaving the doors and windows open is a bad idea when you're going on vacation. Then I tell them that the Pawns are like the walls of the house and should be kept up, except to let the pieces out to play.

In week three, I teach the Queen. Because the Queen combines the movements of the Rook and the Bishop, it's naturally next.

I want them to practice the hand/eye coordination it takes to get the piece from the square it's on to the square where they want it to go. I want them to know how to take opponents' pieces and how it feels to be captured.

In week four, they get the King, and with it, check and checkmate. It's a big step to go from moving and capturing to recognizing that the King is in danger and saving it.

On week five they are taught the Knight. I usually save it for last because it has the most complicated movement, two squares in one direction and one in another. I have a favorite trick to teach the Knight: I call it the Knight's Dance. I put the new people in a row and make them physically move their bodies like the Knight moves. *Hop, hop, hop. Hop, hop, hop.* We do it forward. We do it sideways. We do it backward. I trust the kinesthetic sense to get the point across.

In the sixth week, we go through the promotion of Pawns and castling rules, and the learning phase is complete.

> **All things are easier to absorb in small bites. You can choke trying to swallow the whole thing at once. It's similar to learning two plus two before tackling long division. To synthesize the chunks into a big picture is a learned skill and takes practice. You must recognize that the forest exists, but until you examine the trees you won't know what resources are at hand.**

Yes, they've been playing with some pieces, one or two having been added to their games each week; but until all the pieces are in the game, they're not playing chess.

No matter what the age of the student (older students complete this learning stage in only a couple of classes), the change from playing incomplete chess games to actually engaging in a real game is both exciting and stressful. Many times, I will pair an experienced opponent with a newbie, with the idea that the experienced player will be able to tell me whether the new player has a true grasp of chess playing. This pairing can bear interesting results.

As the kids play, I walk around the classroom and observe the games in progress. This is what I do all the time. This is how I keep track of who knows what and discover what to teach to the individual students, because from this time onward, that's how I teach—talking to a specific child for a specific reason.

At this stage, I'm paying particular attention to the new people in order to assess their levels of understanding. It may be that one of the children has captured nearly all of the pieces of the other, and I ask how that happened. Did you get captured and not take back? Did you fail to keep your pieces protected, so that when you were captured you could not take back? These are the only two valid reasons for this imbalance to have occurred. It presents a teaching opportunity.

Then, more spectacularly, I may encounter a position where the newbie is in check and is staring forlornly at the board.

"Are you in check?" I ask.

"Yes," the newbie will answer. "I lost." The child is despondent.

"Why do you say that you lost?" I continue.

"My opponent says I lost," the poor child answers.

You might be thinking I should address the child proclaiming that their opponent has lost the game. But that's not how I approach it. I want to teach the poor deceived child not only how to spot the deception, but to counter it. That is by far the more important lesson here.

"If you agree that you've lost, then you've lost," I say. "Everybody loses. It's okay to lose a game, if you've really lost it. It's not okay to lose a game you haven't really lost, but only lost because you gave up. So, before we get to that, let's take a look at the position.

"You are in check, correct?" I ask and get a nod from the student. "Which piece is giving check?" The poor child points to the attacker.

"Can you capture the piece that's giving check?" I pause to allow the child to assess and answer.

"Can you stick another piece in between to make a wall?" Pause again. Wait again.

"Can you move the King away?"

The sad kid is barely looking at the board, and I may have to repeat the questions a little more loudly and forcefully, usually with stress on the key to getting out of the desperate situation. I never give up and walk away. I do give the student all the time they need to wrench themselves out of the mindset of losing and into one where they seek a solution.

Eventually, I'll get the child to actually look at the position on the board analytically, and then I go through the questions again, waiting for an answer to each before moving to the next. Can you capture the attacking piece? Can you stick something in between? Can you move the King away? Occasionally the child has been so blinded by the words of the opponent they do not see the obvious and give incorrect answers to the three simple questions.

I ask again, "Can you capture the piece that's giving check? Did you look at all your pieces? Can you capture it with this piece? (I point to a piece that cannot capture.) Can you capture it with this piece?"

I continue to point to pieces until we come to the one that can indeed capture the attacking piece, and finally the student comes to the conclusion that it is not checkmate. Another example would be if the piece can't be captured, but the King can move away. In this case, I would point to each square to which the King might move in order to determine whether that move is legal, I continue to do so until the student correctly analyzes the position.

This is where I come to the good part.

"NEVER believe your opponent," I say forcefully. "Your opponent is trying to win. If they can get you to give up, they win. NEVER believe your opponent!"

Then I turn to the class and ask: "Class, should you believe your opponent?"

The class as one responds by shouting: "NEVER believe your opponent."

It's a phrase they all know well.

I continue speaking to the formerly forlorn child.

"Never believe your opponent. Your opponent is trying to win. Maybe they're right; maybe they're wrong. Use your own brain. Do not use your opponent's brain. Your opponent is trying to win."

If I've gotten through to the student, I can see a light go on and they capture the attacker, or put a piece between the attacker and the King, or move the King out of harm's way—whichever of the three gets them out of check—and the game continues. Lesson learned!

> **Now, here's the real-life lesson. We meet opponents in many situations where we don't necessarily expect them, and not only on the chessboard. Anyone who is trying to sell you something is an opponent and can make their product sound indispensable. Should you believe the sales pitch? Use your own brain. Your opponent is trying to win.**
>
> **Anyone who is trying to get your vote is an opponent. Should you believe them? Maybe they're right, maybe they're wrong, but they are certainly trying to win. Use your own brain. Gather your own independent information, analyze it, and decide for yourself.**

CHESS VALUES
OR
HOW TO DECIDE WHAT'S IMPORTANT

What's the idea? *The idea here is to teach the student, through both parables and hard numbers, how to determine value and use that knowledge to win the game.*

IN THE CLASSROOM, THERE ARE some things I do specially for my youngest children, like giving them mazes and reward stickers. In the first session, I give the new kids tiny stickers for a correct answer. I put these stickers on noses, shoes, buttons, or other unusual places. If a child loses the sticker, I don't give a replacement; but after I give it to them initially, I do tell them that they are responsible for its care.

I give the tiny stickers for correct answers only in the first session. After that, the youngest are awarded one, and only one, sticker at the end of the hour, and I affix it to the completed maze just before they leave the classroom. I am not a believer in endless rewards. They become meaningless and pointless very quickly. I want the children to realize that when they get a reward from me, they have *earned* it.

Instead of endless reward stickers, I will give the students an opportunity to feel the pleasure of accomplishment, and one way to do that is to instruct them in the fine art of poster-making. This gives the kids a way both to reinforce lessons they've learned and to hand their parents a really big and tangible accomplishment. The younger the child is, the more impressive the completion of the poster becomes.

It's poster day for my youngest new students. The old kids have already made their posters in courses past, but the new ones don't quite know what "making a poster" means. After the chess-playing part of the class, I gather them at the art table and pass out large sheets of paper, which I have pre-ruled with six lines; but I only give them to the new students.

I select one new child to stand at an easel so everyone can see what they are supposed to be doing, and I give directions for each of them to make a personal poster. The old children may either supervise and aid the youngest of the new ones (pre-pre-K is just learning the alphabet or may not know it at all) to create the poster, or they may do their usual mazes if they prefer.

It's the only time I allow them to use markers, because using a pencil would render the writing too faint to be seen easily, and I don't care about the penmanship. The result I'm looking for is shown below:

Pawn	=	P	=	1
Bishop	=	B	=	3
Knight	=	N	=	3
Rook	=	R	=	5
Queen	=	Q	=	9
King	=	K	=	∞

The students write the name of the piece (i.e., Bishop); show the letter by which they are identified, in both algebraic and descriptive notation (the two chess languages); and give the value of the piece (B = 3). If you don't know much about chess, you may be puzzled by the term "value of the piece." Each chess piece has a relative exchange value, based on its intrinsic power on the board.

Early in course, when I'm teaching how the pieces move, I put, for example, a Knight in the center of the board. Then I ask a student to place a piece on the board where the Knight might move—either one of the same color as the Knight (which the Knight is then protecting), or one of the other color (which the Knight is then attacking). I continue to call students up to place a piece until all six possible squares are filled. Then I ask what shape they see.

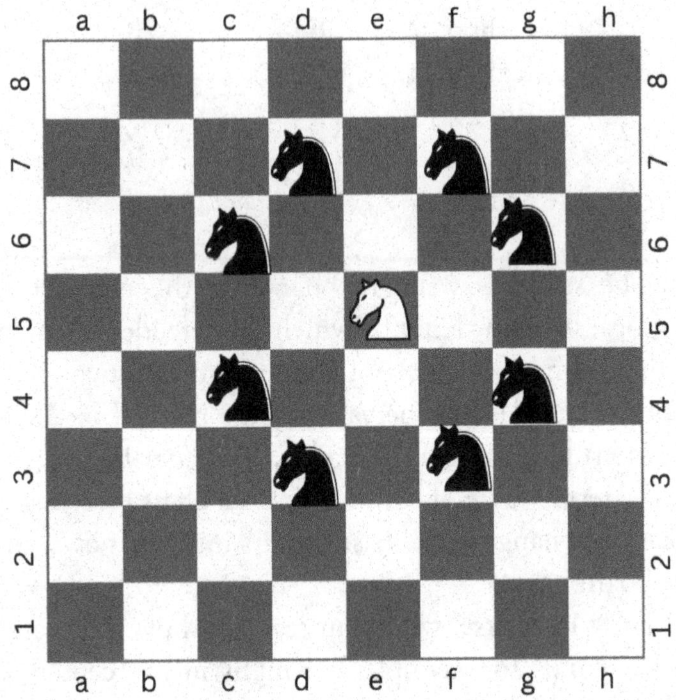

I do the same for other pieces, but the Queen has the most interesting shape of movement. It's a starburst that covers twenty-seven squares, nearly half the board.

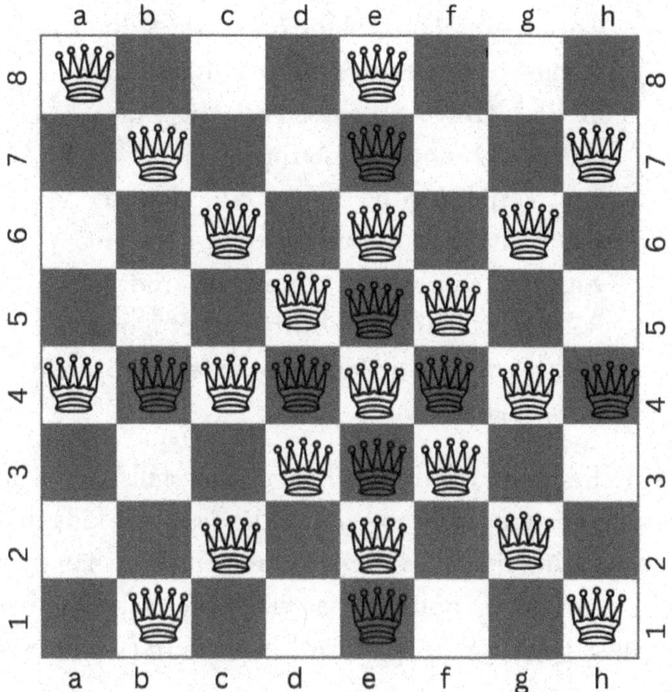

The Pawn influences three squares, the one on which it sits and the two diagonally ahead of it. That's why it's only valued at 1, and why the Queen, which influences twenty-seven, is valued at 9.

The relative values of the pieces give a price for each one, which can help the player decide if captures are to their benefit or not. In chess, we call the pieces on the board *material.* Their values also aid in deciding how to protect your material and may determine who wins the game if time runs out.

What are the assets in your life, and how would you place a value on them? What things or attributes help you to win in life? Don't consider just the material assets; they sometimes are of the least value to your life overall. How do you assign a value to the things within yourself, things that cannot be traded? Relationships? The ability to get along with people? To lead people? To rationally analyze data?

In chess, the relative exchange value tells us if you are making an even or uneven trade. I tell the kids that in any trading situation they want to get more than they give up, or at least not lose material value. Whoever has the most material on the board has a better chance of winning the game.

Before we get to that, however, I must persuade the students that trading chess pieces is a good thing. Kids who have a good knack for chess revel in the capture. For others, especially (but not only) the girls in the class, the concept of capturing is not difficult to understand, but is very difficult to implement. Their initial impulse is to hold onto their own pieces by placing them where they think they are not in danger. Moreover, they are reluctant to capture the pieces of their opponents. It's as if they have moral objections to it.

Not capturing is not a winning strategy. The more pieces on the board, the bigger the number of possible moves in response, and those numbers can be astronomically high. The fewer pieces on the board, the easier it is to see threats or possibilities. I try to drill the concept of trading into their analysis. I repeat over and over: you can't play chess without capturing and being captured. For some, my repetition isn't enough.

These kids counter an opening move of a Pawn to the center of the board (one of the easiest ways to start a chess game) with a Pawn move to the flank. If I ask why they're making that move, they often respond by telling me, "So it can't be captured." Sometimes they want to open a door for the Rook to exit. It's very hard to convince them otherwise. Only by losing the game, or several games for that matter, will they gradually come to realize that opening flank moves are crummy and that trading pieces is a good thing, as long as you keep the trades even or get more than you give up.

That's the great thing about chess. The results of your decisions are manifest immediately, which is of immense help in teaching students how to make good decisions. I can demonstrate on the spot that, for good or for bad, *this* happened because you did (or didn't do) *that*.

This is where I have to instruct the students on what I mean when I say, "Keep your pieces protected." Pieces are protected when two or more work in concert. Being protected doesn't mean you are safe from attack. It means that if you are captured, you can take back. In chess, trades must happen. By allowing my pieces to be captured in instructional games, I show them that you can protect a piece from an opponent's piece of the same or higher value, but you can't protect it from a lower-valued piece. As I tell my students all the time, if your protected Bishop is attacked by an opponent's Queen, *whoopee!* Let them take it, because when you take back, you gain material, giving up three but getting nine.

In baseball, football, soccer, indeed, most sports, you are either playing offense or defense, but not both at the same time. In chess, you must be offensive and defensive simultaneously. Chess pieces are a team, even if the chess player is solitary. The pitcher can't win a baseball game alone; it takes nine players on the field. In this sense, the chess player is more like a manager who shepherds the pieces to win.

I try to drill into their analysis the concept: you can't play chess without capturing and being captured. I repeat over and over: if someone takes one of your pieces, take back! A portion of my new students will never be willing to do so.

> **If you don't want to get punched in the nose, don't go in for boxing. If you are squeamish about bashing a leather-covered ball with a wooden bat, don't play baseball. If you are unable to accept rejection, don't become a writer. If you can't accept having your material captured, or capturing opponent's material, you can never play chess.**

CHESS IS A BIG NUMBERS GAME OR GAME, ART, SCIENCE

What's the idea? *The massive amounts of information available in today's world are overwhelming. For this reason, the student must learn to narrow their scope in order to solve any problem. This section shows this immensity and discusses how chess patterns help the player to focus on what is practical.*

Just wait until you see their faces as they calculate the grains of rice on the chessboard. It will make your day.

CHESS IS MORE THAN A game. Chess is art, with the appreciation of skill to produce the beautiful. If you've never seen a beautiful combination of chess moves, or an aesthetically pleasing checkmate, well, you'll just have to take my word for it. If you wish to appreciate chess from an aesthetic viewpoint, I encourage you to study the games of the chess greats. They are widely available on the internet. Once you know the chess languages (mainly algebraic notation, but also the older descriptive notation), literally centuries of the best chess players' work in the known universe are open to you.

Search for the games of Bobby Fischer to see for yourself. You'll find beauty, I assure you. In addition to being highly instructive, his sharp, surprising moves have brought me much joy. I've spent many happy hours playing over Fischer's games, by myself and with my students. Because of how young Bobby was when he played the games recorded in his *My 60 Memorable Games* book, they are especially relevant to the kids in my classes. Additionally, the fact that he grew up a local Brooklyn boy, learning to play at the Grand Army Plaza Library, within walking distance of Park Slope brings him to neighborhood icon status.

Chess goes beyond both game and art, in that one can also argue it is science. Chess organizes facts (the moves and rules) into systematic and meaningful patterns, which are developed as a result of experimentation. This last statement describes exactly what chess is. Winning patterns have been established through trial and error (isn't that experimentation?) over the course of millions of games played.

Chess is art, game, and science all rolled into one. That's why it not only has endured through the millennia, but also has grown, developed, matured, been refined. That's why it has an audience of millions from all parts of the globe. That's why two people who've never met each other or even speak the same language are able to sit face to face and compete over a chessboard for fun. Grandfathers teach grandchildren in order to bond. Women can play against men. Chess clubs form communities worldwide. Local as well as international tournaments are held.

When you find an activity as popular and long-lasting as chess, you have to ask why this is so. It's my opinion that chess crosses all the lines mentioned above and can be enjoyed casually or so seriously that people devote their lives to it. A popular aphorism states: "Chess is an ocean from which a flea can drink and an elephant can bathe."

There are things that bring us together, and chess is one of them.

How and when was chess created? There's an apocryphal story I enjoy telling my students. Here it is:

Once upon a time, long, long ago, in about the year 450 CE, in a land called Persia, which we now call Iran and India, there lived a very, very, very rich king. In the language of the country, the king was called a Shah. Shah means king in Persian. This Shah was so very, very rich he had everything in the universe he ever wanted. Nothing was new or different to him, and as a result, the Shah was bored.

The Shah called together the wisest and most intelligent men in his kingdom and asked them to create a game for him to play. The wise men (for at that time they were all men) left the Shah and went home to think. Soon one returned with a game he just knew the Shah would like.

The wise man called the game *Chaturanga*, which, in the language of the country, meant "four arms." It was played by two people on a board of sixty-four squares of alternating colors, just like chess is today. It had sixteen pieces, although some were different from the pieces we use today. For example, instead of Rooks, Chaturanga had elephants, and the Queen was called the Counselor and had a more limited scope of movement.

After the wise man taught the Shah to play Chaturanga, the Shah was so pleased he offered the wise man any prize he desired. The wise man thought and thought and asked the Shah to give him one grain of rice on the first square of the board, to double it on the second, and again on the third, and so on until it had been doubled for all sixty-four squares.

The Shah laughed, thinking, "This so-called wise man gives me this great diversion, and all he asks as a reward is a bag of rice." With that, the Shah ordered his accountants to tally the bag of rice and deliver it to the wise man. The accountants went off to calculate the prize, but soon returned with bad news. The amount of rice necessary was so incredibly high, the price could never be met.

At this point in the story, I instruct my students to double the grains of rice for only two of the eight files on the chessboard. That number, unbelievably, turns out to be 32,768! That's only the number of rice grains on the sixteenth square. Adding all sixteen together, you get the unbelievable number of 65,535 in total for the first sixteen squares. If you were to continue doubling for the remaining six files, and then adding them together, the number you would get is:

18,446,744,073,709,551,615

Or: eighteen quintillion, four hundred forty-six quadrillion, seven hundred forty-four trillion, seventy-three billion, seven hundred nine million, five hundred fifty-one thousand, and six hundred and fifteen.

I usually end this tale by saying that the Shah could never pay the wise man and so had him killed. The wise man, who might have had any gift in the world, asked for the impossible. He wasn't so wise after all.

There are other variants of this story, and recent research suggests that the game of chess was invented in China and might well be older than the 1,600 years in this tale, but we don't know for sure.

We are a numbers culture. Numbers describe all aspects of our society. We are used to dealing with very large numbers—just think of our national debt—but the numbers we regularly come across in chess are large enough to boggle even our numerically numb minds. They give insight to why chess is so endlessly fascinating. It's always

the same, yet, like snowflakes, always different.

If this were the end of the "Chess is a Big Numbers Game" story, it would surely be enough, but it isn't the end. There's more to come.

In the first ten moves of any chess game, there are more possibilities of variants than there are stars in the sky or grains of sand on all the beaches in the world. To be clear, it's estimated that there are 1,000,000,000,00 0,000,000,000,000 stars in the sky.

Consider only the first moves for White and Black. For White, there are twenty first-move possibilities. Each of the eight Pawns can move one square or two squares, or sixteen possible moves. Additionally, each Knight can move to two different squares, or four possibilities. This means White has a choice of twenty different first moves.

Now consider that for every one of those twenty possibilities, Black has a choice of twenty responses. The numbers get really big really fast, just like the grains of rice pile up quickly on the chessboard.

Over the course of a millennia, chess players have discovered and verified that certain opening patterns work better than others, and that some endgame patterns are confirmed inevitably by checkmate. King and Pawn endgames are, in fact, mathematical. There is no

> **further experimentation necessary. Similarly, as a civilization we have discovered certain patterns lead most often to happiness and success. Becoming addicted to heroin is not a path to either happiness or success. Learning to think effectively and completing your education (whether academic or vocational) puts us on a much better course.**

Lastly, I could not end this discussion without mentioning that, unlikely as it seems, chess, music, and mathematics all have something in common. Each produces prodigies. Very, very young children can succeed in mastering them. Think Bach, Beethoven. Think Gauss. Think Jose Raul Capablanca. Think Fabiano Caruana.

There is a simple reason for this. Neither math, nor music, nor chess require verbal skills.

So much of academic culture is centered on verbalization or written explanation. How many children are left out of academic success because they lack verbal skills? Having worked with English-as-a-second-language kids, I know this is so. I only have to think of Robert, whom I mentioned earlier, a true chess and math whiz. Robert's mother is an immigrant from Ecuador and his father is an immigrant from Columbia, and so Spanish is spoken in the home. Even though Robert attended a magnet school for gifted children, he failed to gain admittance to the gifted program, because he lacked the verbal skills needed to test well. If you asked a young Robert a question, he invariably answered monosyllabically, and yet he taught me a very valuable lesson when he was in kindergarten.

Because he had to travel a few miles to attend my class at Congregation Beth Elohim, Robert arrived late for some classes. I knew he could play the game, but I had always failed to understand how well he played it until one fateful day. Since he had arrived late to class, the other children were already paired off, and I chose him to play me. I made a move, left the board, and circulated around the room. When I returned, I made another move and repeated the procedure four times. When I walked away that last time, I heard Robert announce:

"Checkmate, Ms. Carol!"

I had realized Robert was trying to use a popular four-move checkmate to win the game, but what I didn't see was that he was prepared to sacrifice one of his Knights to get the job done.

That day, I underestimated the ability of a kindergartner for the last time.

HOW TO BE A GOOD WINNER OR GOOD GAME. I HAD FUN.

What's the idea? *Winning and losing don't only apply to game-playing. You win when you get into the college of your choice or get the job you wanted. This chapter discusses how to instruct your student to win graciously.*

THERE ARE TEN CHESS GAMES being played. The noise level in the classroom makes it sound as if you're teaching on a runway at JFK International Airport. Kids are laughing, standing, fidgeting, singing, and maybe dancing. I have to speak rather loudly to be heard as I walk board to board to assess the progress of the games and to offer instruction, as needed. I have to be careful not to tip the balance of any of those games on which I comment.

It's nearly five fifteen, and the second class of the day (third, fourth, and fifth graders) is winding down. The kids are tired, hungry (even though they've had snacks), and, as my mom would say, over-excited. I know some of these games will be resolved naturally and some will not; but all of them must end soon, the sets will have to be properly bagged, the kids will need to get their things together, and my assistant will have to assign kids to carry stuff down to the school's office for storage until next week. At least four kids are calling my name, and I've had a week's worth of aerobic exercise in the past two hours.

I must see the end of each chess game. That's the rule in all my classes. I want to eyeball all checkmates. Most importantly, I want to make sure they *are* checkmates, and if they are not, to instruct the student on the losing end about what to do, by means of judicious questioning.

> **Identify your problems and check for solutions that are certain. Determining what is true is of vital importance so you can proceed logically. There are many instances where establishing the truth is difficult, sometimes impossible, and it's necessary to make a best guess. In chess, it is theoretically possible to find the truth, but sometimes the number of possibilities is so high that only a computer can calculate them. In certain instances—the endgame, for example—it is possible to calculate the truth, just as we do in math.**

However, whether you've won or lost, shake hands, say "Good game, I had fun." Then reset the pieces and play another.

Additionally, I want to see the end of all games in order to know what kind of checkmates are being used, thereby learning more about the methods of the winner and the deficiencies of the loser. And so I am running from board to board, closing down the games.

For each side of the game there are three possible outcomes. You can win. You can lose. Or the game can be a draw. At the end of a class, for games that have not ended naturally, I determine a winner by the position on the board. This is called adjudication. If one of the kids has an overwhelming advantage, such as being up a Queen, or having a checkmate pattern I know they can solve, it's easy. The winner is obvious. If the position is less clear, I am the final judge, and I must maintain my reputation of being fair. This is the reason for the firm rules governing the resolution of chess games based on time limitations.

Rules are rules for a good reason. When applied fairly, they create an atmosphere of peace and trust. Rules are especially important to children, and consistency in their application makes everyone feel safe.

You must have six points more than your opponent on the board in order to be declared winner. The points are determined by counting the relative values of the pieces left on the board: nine for the Queen, five for each Rook, three for each of the Knights and Bishops, and one for each Pawn. To avoid error, I require the players to calculate the numbers for both sides, and then we can tell if anyone has won the game.

If one side has five or fewer extra points—say, a Bishop and two Pawns, or a Rook, or five Pawns—then the game is a draw. Nobody wins. Nobody loses. There are very rare occasions when one side can demonstrate that checkmate will be forced in a couple of moves, but these are exceptions, not the rule. The vast majority of cases are accepted without argument.

There are almost never hard feelings concerning the adjudication of a chess game. The rule is hard and fast. The rules for winning and losing in my classes are also well known. It is also very rare that any student cries or acts out when they lose, because I have taught them, drilled into their little brains, the correct way to win a game.

No one—repeat, no one—is ever allowed to gloat when they win. No one is ever allowed to brag when they capture a Queen, or have an overwhelming position. The first time they do gloat or brag, I call them outside of the classroom for "a little talk."

I tell them, in no uncertain terms, that kind of behavior is never acceptable in my class. I tell them their opponent knows they've lost the Queen or lost the game, and that they do not have to be told, and the rest of the class doesn't have to be told, either. I tell them it's okay to feel good when you win. It's okay to go home and tell mom or dad or grandpa or Uncle Joe how wonderful you were in chess today. It's not okay to embarrass your opponent or make them feel bad.

I ask how they would feel if the shoe was on the other foot. I remind them they are not the best players in the world and there are plenty of people who might beat them. I teach that when you win a game, that's the time to be kind to your opponent. You've already won the game, and it's now the time to find something nice, not mean, to say. Every game must end with a handshake and the words:

"Good game. I had fun."

Conversely, no one who has lost a game is allowed to act out. I tell them that everybody loses. Even the New York Yankees win just over half their games. I am quick to point out the things they did right, by saying things like: "You fought to the very end and you showed a lot of courage." I show them how they have improved since their previous game and encourage them to keep getting better.

Everybody loses. The important thing is to learn from your losses, to make them meaningful, to use them to help you grow. Ask yourself why you lost. What were your mistakes? How can you do better in the future? Furthermore, no one ever gets better in chess by play-

ing only those people whom they can beat. The only way to get better is to play better players.

I have found it indisputable that good winners make for good losers.

TOUCH MOVE OR ACTIONS HAVE CONSEQUENCES

What's the idea? *Actions have consequences. The exercise recounted here demonstrates how to lead your students to be more cautious before they act, so as to produce better outcomes. These are hard exercises, and difficult lessons to learn.*

The touch-move rule is the culmination of all the other lessons taught thus far. It requires acquiring data, analyzing it, and implementing that information effectively to reach the desired goal.

IT'S ANOTHER BEAUTIFUL DAY. PERHAPS it's raining, it doesn't matter. I'm in a classroom full of robust, chess-playing kids and am having a great time. All of a sudden, the words ring out:

"Touch move!"

I turn and see one of my students, arm outstretched, finger pointing directly at his opponent. He might as well have been saying *"J'accuse!"* His opponent is holding a Black Rook suspended over the board, and the look on his face is a cross between guilt and surprise. I, however, am not surprised. The accuser is doing exactly as I have taught.

So these kids are playing a game of chess, one of eight or nine being played in my class. It's the turn of the player with Black to move, and that's the player with the grip on a Black Rook. He had been loudly discussing the position with his opponent and anyone else who cared to listen. The player with the White pieces has just discovered, but hasn't mentioned, the fact that no matter where the Rook is legally placed on the board, it's going to be captured. The looks on both my students' faces tell me all I need to know. The kid holding the Rook is now doing his best to look innocent; his opponent can't help but vacillate almost imperceptibly between a smile and a grimace.

Now the player holding the Rook is looking for a good place to put it down. Maybe if the Rook started on d8 instead of e8, a safe square might be found. Maybe no one will notice, or his opponent won't mention the slight shift. Maybe. Maybe he just might be able to argue himself out of the pickle.

The player with the White pieces has recognized an opportunity to win an opponent's Rook and takes advantage of the situation by calling "touch move."

The touch-move rule states that if it's your turn to go, and you touch a piece on the board, you must move it; if you release that piece from your grasp, it must remain on the square where you let go, regardless of the consequences. If you've touched a piece, even if you've moved it to a legal square, then as long as you haven't let go of it, you can relocate that piece to another square. It's even permitted to return the piece to the square from which it started, let go, and reconsider where to place it; however, that piece must be moved.

> **It's much easier to identify potential problems before they occur than to try to rectify them afterwards. When the impending difficulties are caught early, we can minimize the impact. If we wait until the piece is actually dropped, it becomes a he said/he said (or he said/she said, or she said/she said) situation, and arguments result.**
>
> **When we began to do mazes, I taught the children how to identify errors after they occurred and to fix them. Then we learned to avoid them by tracing the route with our fingers before committing to a pencil. When the touch-move rule is called, we're simultaneously working to prevent problems before they occur and taking the chance to gain materially. It's profitable to see an opportunity in the making and seize the day. The player with White wanted to capture the Rook and**

> **saw how to implement the touch-move rule to do so.**
>
> **The ability to look ahead is priceless to any serious thinking.**

This is the crux, the heart of the matter, the touch-move rule. The touch-move rule isn't found in the official rules of chess. It is more like a convention accepted in all chess tournaments, in serious play, and definitely in all my classes (as soon as the students are able to play a complete game).

Beginner chess players think with their fingers. They want to handle Bishops, Knights, Rooks, Pawns, and especially Queens and Kings. They want to fondle them, to pet them as they would a doggie. They want to pick them up off the board, hold them aloft, and then put them back down, optimally on the square on which they originated. Then they want to pick up another piece and do the same. In fact, they will do this serially to every piece as they consider them, if they are allowed to do so. If that were allowed, it would mean there would be multiple opportunities for multiple pieces to "accidentally" shift to different squares. That's a big no-no.

I do not allow it; no good chess teacher would. It's bad for the game and it's bad for the mind. Bruce, for example, tortures his serious students by not allowing them to touch the pieces at all. He makes them play virtually the entire game without touching or moving any pieces at all. They are required to play the game mentally. They must play the game in the same way *The Queen's Gambit's* Beth Harmon plays mental games on the ceiling of her bedroom.

But although the touch-move rule might aid in developing this talent, it's not exactly what the rule was designed to do. There are good, practical reasons for the touch-move rule. For one, and an important one to be sure, it reduces to an absolute minimum the opportunity for less-than-honest play or for honest mistakes. The less pieces are touched, the less chance there is of misplacing one, intentionally or unintentionally.

Additionally, for the opponent of the offender, there is an opportunity to gain material by using the touch-move rule to force a bad move.

I arrive at the board in contention to intervene. I ask the player with the White pieces where the Black Rook was before it was picked up. Then I ask the opponent holding the Rook if that's the correct square. If the players agree it's the correct square, touch move applies, the Rook must be moved, and play continues. If they don't, well, I have a system for dealing with that.

I ask the student with the Black pieces how the Rook arrived on that square, and to do so without moving any pieces on the board, just to use words. If I get an intelligible response, I then ask the player with White the same question. If I don't get an intelligible response from either one of the players as to how the

Rook arrived on the square, my mind is pretty well made up, but I still continue with the questioning.

What I'm doing is asking the students to play the game in reverse, from memory, without actually moving any pieces. Once you begin to move pieces, it becomes impossible to determine the truth. If one of the players cannot or will not recall the moves, or moves any of the pieces on the board, the problem is solved. The student with the most logical reiteration, or who hasn't moved any pieces, is deemed to be right.

> **This method is essentially the same that I use in fixing the mistakes the youngest students make in doing mazes, but in a more elaborate and consequential way. We've built on an established procedure. We all live and learn, using past lessons to succeed in the present. Those who can envision the future based on the present often gain material. Seems obvious intellectually, but to do so in actual life situations is a learned skill which is difficult to master.**

"Piece-connection" is the chess rule which states that if a player whose turn it is to go, is holding a piece intended to move governed by the touch-move rule, and connects that piece to a piece of the opponent, then the opponent's piece must be taken. The pieces have been connected; capture must occur.

Taken together, touch move and piece-connection force the players to thoroughly think through their progress during the game. Beginners often just concentrate on moving the pieces correctly, without thought of a game plan, even one which is only a move or two into the future. They see a square to which a piece can be moved and go to it. Sometimes, too late, they discover the move will bring grief and attempt to remedy the situation by any means possible. It's up to the opponent to see that never happens.

> **Once you've lost your Queen due to touch move, believe me, you are much more careful in the future. Experience is the best teacher.**
>
> **That's why, even if touch move isn't called, instead of addressing the student making the mistake, I talk to the player against whom an illegal move is being made, particularly when the student is new to the game. I ask: is this move legal? I want them to recognize the necessity of monitoring the game in progress and to make sure that if they win or lose, it must be legal. If they are going to lose, it must be because they were outplayed, not because an uncorrected mistake was made. I want them to learn to stand up for themselves, to**

hold to the rules, and to hold opponents accountable also. That's why I was pleased when the student with the White pieces in this tale called "touch move." That child was actually watching the game, recognized an opportunity, and told me about it in a proper manner.

I think these are among the most important things I can teach.

PART TWO

The second part of *Strategic Moves* provides anecdotes demonstrating aspects of instruction aimed at educating the teacher.

GIRLS AND CHESS OR STYLISTIC DIFFERENCES

What's the idea? *You'll remember that kids solved the "make your own chessboard" exercise by various methods. It's necessary to find the unique way to reach each and every particular child. As a teacher, I've found that some, but not all, girls play chess differently from most other people., They approach the game with a distinct style. In this chapter, I have some amusing and informative stories about—oddly enough, as the name implies—girls and chess. You might want to think about this as you try to find the right way for your student to learn.*

I THOUGHT OF TEN DIFFERENT WAYS to begin this chapter, but I finally decided to tell a funny yet poignant story about a girl in a recent chess class. It happened during my last year at PS 107 in Park Slope, just before the pandemic. It was the second session of the day, and the class was composed of third, fourth, and fifth graders, most of whom had previous experience with me.

This particular little girl, a third grader and therefore one of the younger students in the class, had just begun to learn the game. She knew the moves and rules already, but had just started to play real games using all the pieces. She was quiet and a little bit shy, and unlike many of the girls in the class, didn't come attached to any friends. Girls tend to show up in bunches, as if they need each other for support. This one was alone in a sea of kids (90 percent of whom were boys, and older boys at that) who knew me and each other from previous semesters. Any of them would gladly play her because they saw her as an easy win. This intimidated her, as did the noticeable level of noise and blatantly aggressive behavior.

I knew all this, of course, and paired her up with an older but more agreeable boy, one I knew had the patience and empathy to calm her anxieties and give her a chance to play a real game. He did, however, still want to win, but I understood he wouldn't do so by intimidating her. He was just the perfect opponent for her to put into practice the things I had been teaching. He was a good enough player to win the game, but would not scare my girl witless and into tears.

After the pairings, I sat them in a corner of the classroom away from the noisiest groups, and more or less isolated from the prying eyes and running commentary of the older boys. There were a few other girls in that class, girls who were as loud and assertive as the boys and weren't having any problem integrating. My assistant chose their colors and they began to play.

I left them to their game and walked around the room discussing and connecting with the rather large class of about fifteen or sixteen. It was late in the day, nearly five o'clock, and the kids were both over-tired and over-excited. It's a time I have to keep a tight rein on the class. It's very easy for things to spiral out of control.

I recall the sun was setting and that we could see the beautiful sight from a bank of high windows on the third floor, facing west over Brooklyn. That's one thing I love about teaching these late classes. At certain times of the year, we get to see sunset, especially if my classroom is located on one of the higher floors. I call the kids to the windows, and as a group we bask in the colors and beauty. It's one of the things I hope sticks with them. Another lesson I find to be essential: enjoy the moment.

Every once in a while, I passed the game between the girl and her relatively easygoing opponent. He was ahead by a good bit, and she was looking slightly anxious. There wasn't much conversation going on, but it didn't seem like it bothered either of them much, so I mostly kept silent and watched how the game proceeded.

Then, over the din of the class, I heard the word I was expecting.

"Checkmate!"

I walked over to the board to see how it ended. The girl was sitting stock-still, staring at the board, and the boy was smiling but not gloating. Looking down at the position, I saw his Queen face-to-face with her King. It was definitely check. There was one thing he had missed, however: the Queen wasn't protected and could be captured by her King. Check, yes. Checkmate, no. This is where my work started.

She was nearly at the point of concession, a little dejected but not surprised by the outcome. I intervened.

I looked at the boy and quietly told him, "The part that comes next is only for learning. No matter what happens, I want you to know how well you've done. Besides, even if she takes the Queen, you're still ahead by eight points. You'd win no matter what. But right now, I've got to teach your opponent some hard lessons. Okay?"

He agreed and I turned to the girl.

"Let's see if it really is checkmate," I told her. "Remember, if you say it's checkmate, even if it isn't, the game is over and he wins. So, before we agree that it's checkmate, let's make sure."

She didn't even look at me. She stared at the position, but it was clear she couldn't see it, had resigned herself to the end of the match.

I began my analysis, one which I've mentioned previously, but with the question I generally ask last—because the solution to the problem was in the question

I normally ask first, and I wanted to give her the opportunity to think it through herself.

"Can you move the King out of check?"

She shook her head.

"Can you move another piece between your King and the Queen?" Since there wasn't even a square between them, this was a rhetorical question. Again, she shook her head.

"Can you capture the Queen?" The two players simultaneously saw that the King could, indeed, capture the attacking Queen. A look of horror spread across the boy's face. I saw it. Luckily for him, she did not. She just sat staring at the position and remained silent, neither nodding nor shaking her head.

I repeated the question: "Can you capture the Queen?" Again, there was no response, so I continued: "If you can capture the Queen, it's not checkmate, and you haven't lost the game yet. Maybe you can even get a draw! Can you capture the Queen?"

She stayed quietly staring at the chessboard.

"I'll let you think about it for a couple of minutes," I said to her, and to the boy I said, "Be patient. If she can't get out of check, you win." Then I walked away. I returned shortly. They were sitting in the same positions. I gave the boy an appreciative look. He was doing well. He wasn't complaining. He wasn't haranguing her, demanding she move. He wasn't angry or impatient. He knew that all he had to do was to wait, and if she didn't capture the Queen, he would de facto win the game. I was impressed by him.

"Well," I said to the girl, "can you capture the Queen?" She still said nothing, so I took her by her hand and led her out of the classroom and into the hall, where we sat on the stairs and I began one of my "little talks."

The gist of the conversation (if you can call it that, because although I spoke, she said virtually nothing) was that in chess it's okay to capture pieces, it's even necessary. You can't play this game without capturing or being captured. You don't have to feel bad when you capture, just be polite. It's okay.

She had been looking down at her hands, and now she looked up at me. I could see that she understood my words, but was not yet ready to do what was necessary to play chess. Then we stood up and went back into the room and she sat back down at the board, but still didn't make the necessary move. Her opponent still waited patiently.

Class was winding down. Most games were over and several of the students had come to watch the game between my little girl and her opponent. They were not as subtle as I was. One or two came over to whisper: *take the Queen!* She didn't. The voices of the kids grew more numerous, louder and louder: TAKE THE QUEEN! This continued for several minutes until the end of the class, when the boy stood up and left the board and the classroom. He left happy. He hadn't lost his Queen or the game.

That's when she, finally, took the Queen.

> **Of course, there are girls who have no problem whatsoever in competing against other girls or boys, for that matter. Take, for example, a young woman I'll refer to as Ms. Z the Younger, who started taking chess classes at The Berkeley Carroll School when she was in pre-K. Right from the onset she was able to sit across from any opponent and compete, having learned to play the game from a classmate—another girl, whom I'll call Ms. J. Like Ms. Z the Younger, Ms. J was poised and confident, even at her tender age. It's a teacher's or parent's job to identify which kind of student is in front of you, and act accordingly.**

There's another interesting side to the girls-playing-chess phenomena. As I said earlier, it often happens that girls come to my classes in bunches. They do quite fine during the instruction that happens early in the term, interacting with understanding and even humor, but things change when the playing starts. Friends who attend chess together will naturally want to play each other. This I have now outlawed, and I can tell you why.

The first time it happened, two friends were playing each other, as I walked around the classroom as usual. Suddenly I heard one of them call out:

"Ms. Carol, we have no more moves left."

That was an odd thing to hear. Have no more moves left? Not "Ms. Carol, checkmate"? I went to investigate. When I observed their game, I saw all of their pieces crowded into the center of the board. No piece had been captured even though many, if not all, could be captured, and the King was in check. The two girls had made all the moves, but refused to take any of their friend's pieces.

The first time it happened, I thought it was funny and had to keep my smile in check. I asked whose turn it was to go and made a move for that student, capturing one of her opponent's pieces. I then instructed the other student to reply. She made a move, now that there was an available space, but did not capture. I laughed and ended the game.

It would have been an amusing anecdote, except that this episode was just a prelude to a pattern. The exact same scenario played out time after time after time, until I instituted the no-playing-your-friends rule. I ruled these girlfriends could sit next to each other in order to play other kids, but could not play each other. I've held firm to it for years now.

One of my long-term students, I'll call her T, developed an interesting method for coping with the game. T was now in the third grade and had been coming to chess since the first grade. Unlike many of the girls, T had not come attached to a bunch of friends. She wasn't a great player, but she had a tenacity that was hard to beat.

One day when I was walking home after my classes were finished, I ran into T, her mom, and her little sister. Since they live around the corner from me, we had a nice long talk. The two girls ran ahead, leaving T's mom and me alone. I started to tell her how great T was doing, but that last week she lost a close game, and I had to have a "little talk" with her. In that talk, I reminded her that she was a third grader playing against a fifth grader. It would have been nice if she won, but she hung on for almost forty-five minutes and never quit. In my opinion, that was more important than winning any one game. That was a life accomplishment, one that would help her for years to come.

The mom looked at me, and that look wasn't as pleased as I had hoped. Then she told me how she had been trying to talk T into taking more glamorous classes, like dance or fashion design. T wouldn't be budged, however. I was surprised at mom, but awed by T's attitude, and I mentally vowed to support her with good advice.

The next week I had a private conversation with T and told her an old story about a former World Chess Champion, Emanuel Lasker, who had an interesting tactic for winning chess games. He would come to play in the big tournaments smoking a big, stinky cigar and blowing smoke into his opponent's face, just to be annoying. Of course, I said, I'm not advocating she take up smoking cigars, but that, given her tenacity and steadfastness, maybe she might find some other diversion for her opponents.

T found one, and she found it with no further help from me. She slowed down all her moves. I mean, she really slowed down her moves. Since thinking is allowed, I could not in good conscience tell her to make her moves quickly, no matter how often or loudly her opponents demanded it. T would think, consider her options, stand up and walk around the board to appraise all sides of the position, feint moves, and generally annoy her opponents with delays. Before long, she had them jumping up and down in frustration and yelling: "MOVE! WOULD YOU MOVE?" This state of mind did absolutely nothing for their chances of winning.

T had found a really effective tactic. She didn't win many games, but neither did she lose many. She did, however, amass a whole bunch of draws and had great fun doing it.

My last girl's story involves a long-time student, former assistant, and friend, Ms. Z. Ms. Z is the younger sister of another memorable student, Mr. G. I first met her when her brother was in my class and she was in a stroller. Ms. Z entered my class in kindergarten and stayed through the fifth grade. She succeeded in winning a year-long bughouse tournament, mainly by integrating into an extremely lively class through a combination of humor and intelligence. When she was in middle school, Ms. Z assisted me teaching the younger students, and continued to do so through high school.

I ran into Ms. Z and her mom during the pandemic. She had just graduated college. I knew she had graduated with a degree in physics, and when I asked what she intended to do with it, Ms. Z told me she wanted to teach. I couldn't have been more pleased. As the conversation continued, she eventually raised the question of what I thought was the most important thing I could teach girls.

I didn't take very long to answer, because I had thought about it long before Ms. Z asked the question. The most important thing I teach girls, I replied, is how to compete against boys.

I saw a bright light go on in Ms. Z's eyes. She understood.

GOOD ADVICE OR LEARNED FROM EXPERTS

What's the idea? *I learned every day I taught, throughout my chess career. It was the best part of any class. I learned from administrators. I learned from other teachers. I learned from parents. I learned from the kids. I bet there's plenty you can teach me, but right now, here are some enlightening episodes you may enjoy.*

OVER THE YEARS, I'VE GOTTEN great advice from both classroom teachers and moms. As a matter of fact, I seek it. There have been times I've asked specific questions and times I've overheard conversations that were helpful. (Yes, being an eavesdropper is sometimes a worthwhile activity.) I listen, I learn.

For example, I listened while a teacher at The Berkeley Carroll School quelled dust-ups by making the kids apologize to each other, and I learned the most effective way to do it.

For the sake of clarity, let's say one kid in my class said the other was stupid, and the second kid gave the first kid a push, which caused him to take a fall. First,

I explain that even an accidental fall can cause death or great harm, if the fall victim hits his head on the edge of a desk or some other sharp or hard thing. I ask: How would you feel if that happened? How would you feel if they started bleeding? Generally, the mention of bleeding gets their attention and remorse. They understand that what they did could easily have become serious.

We never take matters into our own hands, I tell them. If someone says you're stupid, I tell the pair of children, you can ignore them and walk away, knowing you aren't stupid and they are just upset; you can beat them on the chessboard; or you can tell me. You can't shove them to the floor.

The apologies come next. First, the kid who did the pushing says, "I'm sorry for pushing you," then the other one says, "I'm sorry for calling you stupid." Then we shake hands and call the incident finished.

It may seem trivial to say that an apology goes a long way toward making things better, but it does. Most of the time in these situations, it's not a case of one person being mean to another, it's about expressing hurt or anger in an inappropriate way.

As adults we often don't consider saying a sincere "I'm sorry," because saying it is tantamount to admitting guilt. We often don't even consider formally

accepting apologies when offered, because it acknowledges we were hurt.

Both actions are necessary, even if they are uncomfortable.

I think the most important thing I ever learned from a teacher occurred before an afterschool class I was to give at PS 321. Working for years with so many children in so many different classrooms, I had habitually fallen prey to every cold germ in the known universe, and since there were no flu shots available at the time, I came down with a severe case of the flu every year.

This particular time, however, it was allergy season. I sneezed and reached for the box of tissues that was on the window ledge. Every classroom has boxes of tissues on window ledges and shelves, to be readily available to any runny noses in the area. As I reached for one, the in-class teacher gave me a nudge and whispered, "Never take the top tissue."

I immediately understood. There was no way of knowing which grimy, germy little fingers had touched it before me. Not a safe choice. I've never taken the top tissue again, and I'm pleased to report the number and severity of colds I get each year has dramatically reduced, and I haven't had the flu in years, due in part to the flu shots I never miss.

Needless to say, I pass this most valuable information on to all of my assistants.

A stitch in time saves nine, or: never take the top tissue.

Another time, I was giving a private lesson to a very intelligent, gifted, and promising first-grade student I'll call Little Mr. S, when I got schooled by something his mom said. We had finished our lesson and Mom L, as I'll refer to her here, was having a conversation with me about his progress. Little Mr. S had gone into the living room and was watching the nightly news. I don't remember what Mom L was saying to me, but I do recall hearing Little Mr. S call out:

"Mom?"

"Yes?" Mom L responded.

"Do you die if you get shot in the arm?"

Mom L responded quickly: "No."

He continued. "Do you die if you get shot in both arms?"

She again said with certainty: "No."

He didn't give up. "Do you die if you get shot in both arms and a leg?"

Her answer came just as quickly: "No."

Little Mr. S may have continued for a couple more gunshot wounds, I don't remember; but I do remember asking Mom L later on if she really knew whether someone would die after four gunshots.

Mom L replied, "No, I have no idea."

"Then why did you say no?"

"It's important to just answer quickly and definitely."

Amusing, no? And, highly informative. I've used the technique many times over the years—not when the answers mattered, however, but when the questions were trivial, like I was as a child. Gifted kids frequently ask and ask and ask about everything and anything. This is a good thing, but researching every minor point could take over your life. Many times, an educated guess suffices.

My last example of good advice did not come from anywhere in the chess universe. I had just begun to teach and was visiting the home of a friend and neighbor I had known for several years, a middle-aged woman I'll call Mrs. J.

Mrs. J was a widow with four of the best-behaved teenaged children I have ever met. I'd been invited into their home several times for coffee and cake, so I had multiple chances to see them in their own natural environment. There was a near-adult son, twin daughters, and a youngest son, all of whom lived at home. The kids were at prime ages for teenage rebellion, all the more so due to the recent loss of their father. Mrs. J never argued with them or took them to task, and there was never any yelling. When she told them to do something, they did it immediately, with no backtalk or hesitation. They weren't out all hours with their friends, or wearing absurd hairdos. (I always tell parents of teenagers to ignore the funny hairdos, because hair grows back. Likewise, I always tell my students who have grown to be teenagers to avoid anything permanent, like tattoos, piercings, or pregnancies, until they're twenty-one.)

I asked Mrs. J how she did it.

"I talk to them." That was the simple reply, but it did not satisfy me.

"What do you mean, you talk to them?"

"I just talk about what I need them to do, and tell them why I need it, and I keep talking until they finally agree."

When she said this, I thought about how, in the past, I asked endless questions of my instructor. It was really just the opposite side of the coin, wasn't it? Mrs. J said it so simply. No beratement for unacceptable behavior, no shouting—just talking. Oh, and the most important element, the *why* of it. There must be a "because" clause attached, or it doesn't work. Consequences matter.

I put this system into action in my classes whenever I thought it might be helpful, and I found that it worked. Miraculous! That's where I got the "let's have a little talk" method I've mentioned previously.

I also use this system when I enforce the "no flying pieces" rule. It is just what it says: no chess piece is to leave the board and fly through the air for any reason. When anyone tosses or throws any chess piece, whether for reasons of resetting the board or as an act of negative emotion, they get "the talk." This talk has been standardized, rehearsed, repeated over the years. I have it down pat. It goes as follows:

"I've been in classes where someone threw a piece and it hit someone in the eye, or it hit them in the lip and it bled, or they got hit in the tooth and the tooth got broken. No flying pieces at any time. No exceptions."

Commands prompt rebellion. Calmly talking things through is by far the more successful way to achieve cooperation, as long as you explain why. This seems like a trite statement, but it really depends on execution. You need to present clear and reasonable principles for your position, not orders. In my first example, where the two boys got into an insult/pushing match, I could have just said "no pushing" and been done. Instead, I explained the reason for not pushing each other, bringing the conversation into a larger, more applicable scale. When kids understand, they cooperate.

WHAT PARENTS SHOULD NOT DO OR WARNING! WARNING!

What's the idea? *By pointing out the errors of misguided parents, I hope to prevent you from making mistakes of your own.*

I'VE WRITTEN MUCH ABOUT WHAT you should do to get your kids to use their brains, but having taught chess for more years than I care to discuss, I also have lots of examples of what not to do. You'll probably notice these instances involve men and their sons. You shouldn't be surprised, because as a woman in a male-dominated field, my authority gets challenged frequently. Even the little boys will try to steamroll me.

There was one instance of a mother who inadvertently schooled me in handling awkward situations. Her kindergartner threw a screaming tantrum during a Parents' Visitation Day, while she sat smugly on the sidelines and later complained about it to school authorities. I now know I should have led him out of class until he calmed down, but at the time I was new to teaching and had a lot to learn myself.

So, here goes! What follows is my best advice about what parents should *not* do.

Mr. Red Shoes is a new second-grade student in my afterschool class. He had proclaimed loudly and proudly that he knew how to play chess, and my testing verified that fact. When I asked him how he knew how to play, Mr. Red Shoes informed me his father had taught him. I knew immediately there would be a problem, because I had watched this scenario play out many, many, many, too many times before. I hoped against hope that I was wrong, but in my heart of hearts, I knew I would be proven right.

Mr. Red Shoes played a few games against some of the class's mediocre students, and he did well, winning each time and going home with a wide, self-satisfied smile. Then he was matched against one of the class's best students, a third grader I'll call Mr. Sponge Bob Shirt.

I kept track of the game as it progressed and saw Mr. Sponge Bob relentlessly break down Mr. Red Shoes's position. Mr. Red Shoes became increasingly nervous and visibly upset, even though Mr. Sponge Bob wasn't lording it over him. When Mr. Sponge Bob declared checkmate, and it was checkmate, the emotional dam inside Mr. Red Shoes finally broke, and the tears flowed. He was angry, embarrassed, confused. I pulled him outside for "a little talk."

I asked him what was wrong, even though I knew what he would say, because it was the starting point for the conversation he needed to hear.

"I always win. I *always* win," Mr. Red Shoes asserted through his tears. "I beat everybody. I always win."

"Well," I began, "now you're playing really good players, and things are going to change. You're not going to win every game anymore." I wanted to ask if he thought daddy was letting him win, but the last thing he needed right now was to lose faith in his father.

"If you're going to play chess, you're going to lose sometimes. That's just the way it is. If you're not willing to lose, you can never win." I tried to sound as sympathetic as possible. It wasn't the kid's fault. His world image and his confidence had been broken.

"Besides," I continued with a speech I had given students repeatedly, "the best way to improve is to play kids who are better players than you are. You never improve by only playing kids you can beat. You want to get better, don't you? Isn't that why you're here? To learn more about chess?"

Of course, Mr. Red Shoes had to agree with me. What else could he say?

"Go to the bathroom, wash your face, get a drink of water, and when you're ready, come back in."

I give those instructions to every child who is having a hard time coping with the harsh realities of playing chess. It almost always works.

I asked Mr. Red Shoes who taught him to play chess. I ask every new student who tells me they already know the game who taught them to play. If I hear that grandpa taught them, I relax somewhat, because grandpas are generally good teachers. If the answer is that daddy taught them, my Spidey sense tingles, particularly if the new student is a boy. Daddies playing sons is nearly always problematic.

Too many times I've found that daddy as chess teacher goes either one of two ways: either they let their son win all the time, in an attempt to build their relationship and the child's confidence; or they always win, to demonstrate their paternal dominance. Neither is a good strategy. If the former, the kid is in for a rude awakening when he has to play another kid who is trying very hard to win, just like what happened to Mr. Red Shoes. If the latter, the kid is already inured to losing, and, in fact, may expect to lose.

So, to daddies (and mommies as well) the advice I would give is: don't always win; don't always lose. Find a way around the conundrum. For example, play honestly, and when you have achieved a winning position, turn the board around and give your position to your child.

However, the best advice I can give to parents playing against their children, and particularly their sons, is: don't do it, at least not in the early stages of the child's development. Instead of playing each other, I advise the two of you team up to play against a computer program. The chess program can be adjusted to whatever level of difficulty is desired. Always set the level stronger than the child needs to win, so that learning happens. The major advantage of playing against a computer program is that it's less for competition and more for learning.

The program not only allows you to set the level of difficulty, but it lets you take back crummy moves and try to find a better option. Additionally, when the computer achieves a winning position, the board can be turned so that the parent/child team is in charge. These two things, taking back bad moves and turning the board, can be done as many times as needed to complete the game. By using a computer program in this way, the parent and child become a team to defeat a common opponent, instead of competing against each other.

I give this advice to any and all fathers who play chess with their sons, whether or not those kids are in my class. It's that important.

Most afterschool programs have a "Parents' Visitation Day," usually the last day of the term, when the class is open for the students' parents, who are encouraged to attend. It's the only class of the semester that I utterly dread (no offense, parents). First of all, the kids are totally stressed out. On the one hand, they want mommy and daddy to see them play well and win. On the other hand, they are worried that mommy and daddy will see them lose.

The entire situation is fraught with potential for children's tears.

Early on in my career, I was involved in a scenario that led to a huge learning opportunity for me. It was Parents' Day at a small, prestigious private school, and I was running around greeting parents and supervising students who were located in two different classrooms. In one of those classrooms, a fourth-grade boy, a decent chess player, was sitting at a board across from a second-grade girl, who had the potential to be a very decent player. Therein lies the story.

I was in one of the rooms when I heard a disturbance in the other, and I ran back to see what was going on. I found two fathers standing nose to nose—seriously, nose to nose—and they were yelling at each other. The whole room was in an uproar.

It seems that the boy's father had interfered in the game and was telling his son how to beat the young girl. Naturally, and quite rightly, the girl's father objected vigorously. The girl was crying—whether because of what had happened in the game, or because she saw her dad nearly come to blows with another dad, I don't know. The boy was red with shame. His dad didn't trust him to handle a chess game with a younger student.

Now here's the kicker: both men were medical doctors! You'd think they'd know better, wouldn't you?

What goes through the mind of a parent who decides to act in this way, I cannot fathom. The rudeness and self-centered attitude are very apparent and need no comment.

I will speak again to one of the first things I noted in this work. Allow the child to work through the problems without interference. It may take time and mistakes may happen. It certainly takes patience, but that's where the learning and the accomplishment happen. What are you trying to achieve by

inserting yourself into a child's game? Do you want to show you're smarter than your child? How does that help the child to learn or to feel as if they've done something worthy? When they are trying to learn, let them do the work themselves. It's the only way.

The first thing I did in the tense situation cited above was to extricate the girl. The second thing I did was to make up a new rule. The rule I instituted after this incident was as follows:

When a parent enters the class, they should hug and kiss the child, then move six feet away. No standing over the board. No interference of any kind.

Every Parents' Day, I greet each person coming into the room, whether a parent or a caregiver, and cite the above rule. If they've been in my class previously, they already know it. Some of the new attendees get offended. Some ask why, but I have learned through experience that they won't believe or respect my real reasoning. So I have devised an alternate version, which, though true, is really secondary to the prime motive of noninterference.

I tell these parents that the reason to move away is because the children are all keyed up by the arrival of their parents, and that we have to be particularly gentle with those children whose parents were unable to attend, since they are feeling vulnerable. This they generally understand. Generally, but not always.

My last two tales are about parents who did not heed my warnings.

It was Parents' Day (again), and I had handed out simple checkmate-in-one puzzles to the kids, with a small reward (a baseball card) for the student who correctly completed the most first. Checkmate-in-one puzzles give a chess position and allow one move to reach checkmate. I saw one student, who was rather good at solving these puzzles, working away, as were most of the other children. I made a round of the room, and when I turned back, the kid's father was standing over the desk, helping him with the puzzle—this after he had been told about the six-foot rule!

Not one of the other parents was doing anything like this. It forced me to interject myself between him and the child and forcefully suggest he return to the six-foot boundary. Naturally, I had to disqualify the mates-in-one where the father had given help.

The last tale is rather sad. Again, it was Parents' Day. I guess Parents' Day is the best time for me to observe the interactions, and that's the reason these stories are all based there.

A second grader, who had been in my class since pre-K, was already playing chess when his dad entered the room. I had met his mom previously, but the dad had not attended the class before. I greeted him, shook his hand, told him his son was doing well, and gave him explicit six-foot rule standards. I then went off to greet other parents and watch other games. When I returned, having made a full circuit, I found the dad hovering over his son's chessboard. This defied my instructions. I strongly urged him to move away, but he blew me off. I was unable to get through to him and rather than create an ugly scene, I walked away and left it.

When I made my next round, I found the boy sitting alone in the corner, crying, and the father standing sheepishly at the rear of the room. I went over to the boy and tried to comfort him, but with his father watching, I was unable to do so.

Not long after, the class ended. The father and son, who had finally stopped crying, came up to me.

"I'm sorry," the father said. "You were right and I was wrong."

I said as many good things about the boy as I could, and they left. The boy never returned to my class.

Let your children do their own work. Give them the time and space they need to work through the problem. I can't repeat this often enough.

Don't embarrass them in public. You may see yourself as supporting them, but it comes off as if you don't trust or believe in them. If they succeed, praise their efforts. If they fail, stress the best parts of their performance, and urge them forward.

THE GRAND FINALE

What's the idea? *Maybe it's a new world for the education of American youth. Maybe you can make it real, make the change.*

THE PANDEMIC CHANGED MANY THINGS in our lives. Perhaps most significantly for parents, it immersed them into their children's education. They went from just asking "What did you learn in school today?" to watching the lesson in progress—and many, too many, weren't happy with what they saw. Parents began to ask themselves: "Is this the material which will best serve to educate and prepare my child for the future?"

For an uncounted number of them, the answer was no. Parents began to understand the reason for the plummeting reading and math scores. Their reaction was not passive, but active, and they started seeking ways to mold the education of their children in a different model.

The pandemic forced moms and dads into picking up the slack. They were thrust into a position of having to be hands-on with their children's education. This was a change of epic proportions. For generations, parents had relegated more and more of the responsibility for the education of their children to the trusted professionals of the public education system, and, suddenly and without warning, the world turned one hundred and eighty degrees in the opposite direction.

If you have been pushed to new vistas to see first-hand how your children learn and, more importantly, what they are being taught or not taught—if you've decided to regain some control over your children's education—this book is for you. It's my profound hope that non-traditional teachers of all stripes will have found the material presented here helpful in shaping the minds of their students to use logic, to solve problems, and to think proficiently and productively. When children have those skills, nothing is beyond their grasp.

Whether you're a parent helping your child learn what the school has offered, or you're homeschooling them—whether you're an instructor in a brand-new micro school, or you're putting together a group outside of a classroom, or you're running for your local school board—you are making a difference in young lives.

If children didn't learn in the wake of the pandemic as much as they would have during a normal school year, their parents have learned much more than they ever would have. If nothing else, 2020/21 was a banner education year for parents.

My life changed in March of 2020—the last month I gave an afterschool chess class, the last time I worked with kids as a chess teacher, a job I dearly loved. You see, not only did the kids stop going to class in the public schools, all afterschool learning stopped as well. That exuberant wellspring of fun, joy, learning, and thinking dried up in a day. I didn't even get to say goodbye to my students.

Although for decades I taught kids across the intellectual spectrum, in truth, most of the kids who came to my classes fell into the gifted strata, and that's what gave me the most satisfaction, what kept me working year in and year out. Touching those gifted children, helping them reach their best, their highest potential, making them the most useful to society that they can be—that was my goal, my contribution to the future. And it ended abruptly, without warning in March 2020. When I said goodbye to the last class, said "See you next week," there was no way to know there would never be a next week. Then again, life is like that. You just never know.

After more than a century (that is, multiple generations) of ceding increasing control of their children's education to the professionals, moms and dads had the ball thrust back into their unready hands. It had to have been a scary, nerve-wracking moment. Everything was different. Whether they were working at home or not working at all, the onus of their kids' education had to have struck fear into their hearts, as uncertainty often does. Most rose to the challenge, however, and even though it was different, I'm sure they did their best. After all, their children's futures were at stake.

I think the most significant thing that has come out of this for parents is that they now really know how their kids learn, and what the professionals have mandated that they learn. In this book, I'm hoping to have presented methods and practices to assist parents and other non-traditional instructors to teach kids to use their minds in the most effective way possible.

I firmly believe this is the way forward. We cannot rely on the school system to fill all the needs of the children. They have shown they cannot or will not always do so. It's up to you. Will alternatives to mass public schooling become permanent? Will additional enrichment at home or in other venues fill the gaps left by traditional schooling? Only time will tell.

However, you can make a difference. Don't wait for the system to respond to your concerns. Never stop trying to get the response, of course, but use the experiences of the pandemic to move forward independently.

One thing is for sure: the downside of the norm has been exposed, and to many, it's not acceptable. That's the bad. The good? The power previously ceded to the education machine is being returned to the parents.

Now that you have the information, take up the tools to implement changes for the good of the children. Take the opportunity. Use the opportunity. Never give up the power again.

We know the future belongs to the young. It's our job in the present to prepare them for it.

ACKNOWLEDGMENTS

FIRST OF ALL, I MUST acknowledge and thank Bruce Pandolfini, who recognized something in me that I never considered and put my feet firmly on the chess path. I followed it to a long and successful career and enjoyed every single moment I spent doing my job. His constant support and mentoring have been invaluable.

Rebecca Gradinger, my first agent, my neighbor, friend, and mother of one of my most memorable students, saw me sitting on the stoop at the beginning of the COVID-19 epidemic, newly stripped of my career and life's work, crossed the street and asked me what I was doing with all my new found time. I replied I was considering a Podcast. Rebecca immediately replied: "Book first. Podcast second." That was the birth of *Strategic Moves*. Again, someone saw something in me I didn't see in myself.

When Rebecca got a big promotion at United Talent Agency, Kelly Karczewski took over her agent's role and I'd like to acknowledge how great it's been to work with her. Her supportive manner, her expertise in presentation and format, her constant support, quick responses to my cries of "Help!" have been invaluable. She's shared her considerable digital skills with a relative newbie, who didn't even know how to work an editing program on Word.

While I have a substantial background in writing, I've never been through the complex process of publishing a book before. The whole crew at Post Hill Press have eased me through this novelty, from editors Debra Englander, Caitlin Burdette, and Ashlyn Inman to the talented Jim Villaflores, who did the wonderful cover design, to the behind the scenes Tiffany Alexander, Robert Bidinotto, Rachel Hoge, Kate Harris, Alana Mills and Madeline Sturgeon, I can't calculate how much their assistance has been in bringing *Strategic Moves* to market.

ABOUT THE AUTHOR

CAROL ANN CARONIA WAS BORN and raised in Brooklyn and is now living in Park Slope. A graduate of St. John's University, she has pursued a vigorous independent course of study in anthropology, archeaology, history and physics.

Ms. Caronia's career began in business writing, transitioned to business research, then to financial and management roles in nonprofits, and finally to chess, where she spent most of her adult life teaching chess to young children privately and in afterschool enrichment programs, community education centers, and in the classroom.